2015: POWER AND PROGRESS

For sale by the U.S. Government Printing Office
Superintendent of Documents, Mail Stop: SSOP, Washington, DC 20402-9328
ISBN 0-16-048752-8

2015: POWER AND PROGRESS

Edited by
Patrick M. Cronin

National Defense University Press
Washington, DC

National Defense University Press Publications

To increase general knowledge and inform discussion, the Institute for National Strategic Studies, through its publication arm the NDU Press, publishes *Strategic Forums*; McNair Papers; proceedings of University- and Institute-sponsored symposia; books relating to U.S. national security, especially to issues of joint, combined, or coalition warfare, peacekeeping operations, and national strategy; and a variety of other works designed to circulate contemporary comment and offer alternatives to current policy. The Press occasionally publishes out-of-print defense classics, historical works, and other especially timely or distinguished writing on national security.

For more information about NDU Press publications, please call 202/685-4210, or write to NDU Press/INSS, Bldg. 62, 300 5th Avenue, Ft. McNair, Washington, DC 20319, or visit out home page at http:/www.ndu.edu/cgi-bin/wais.pl. Many NDU Press publications are sold by the U.S. Government Printing Office. For ordering information, call (202) 512-1800 or write to the Superintendent of Documents, U.S. Government Printing Office, Washington, DC 20402.

Library of Congress Cataloging-in-Publication Data

Project 2015 : power and progress /Patrick J. Cronin
      p. Cm.
    Includes bibliographical references.
     1. Twenty-first century—Forecasts. 2. World politics—1989-
I.. Cronin, Patrick J., 1952-
CB161.P75 1996
303.49 ' 09 ' 04—dc20   96-19688
                                                          CIP

First Printing, July 1996

CONTENTS

I. WORLD OF GREAT POWERS
Brian R. Sullivan

II. ENVIRONMENT
Patrick L. Clawson

III. COALITIONS
Stephen M. Walt

IV. TECHNOLOGY AND WARFARE
Martin C. Libicki

V. CONCLUSIONS AND RECOMMENDATIONS

FOREWORD

The transition in international relations that began with the unexpected collapse of the Soviet Empire and the huge increase in East Asian economic strength is still unfolding. As is the case in any realignment among the great powers, the ways in which this upheaval will rearrange world politics cannot be foretold in reliable detail. But certain reasonable assumptions about the limits within which states would operate and likely alternatives for the future are possible.

The authors advance a view that is at once familiar and unfamiliar. It is familiar in the sense that great powers would remain the dominant actors in world politics, that failed states or general chaos in the developing world would be unlikely to spark large scale warfare involving the developed world, and that alliances and coalitions would remain only as durable as the common interests on which they are founded. Their view is unfamiliar in the sense that a revolution in military affairs might transform warfare two decades hence principally by tilting the balance between offense and defense. The authors feel that the United States should focus its external policy on relations with the major power centers of the next century, actively encouraging cooperation among the great powers and discouraging developments antithetical to international peace and thus to American interests.

Drawing on the research expertise of NDU's interdisciplinary research arm, the Institute for National Strategic Studies, this work looks ahead to the year 2015 and beyond, seeking to understand how the American armed forces might contribute better to the nation's future security. The authors try to conceptualize how a transformed world situation twenty years from now could affect U.S. security. They describe the most plausible changes likely to develop—not as prophecy nor as an intelligence forecast, but as a considered statement of those recognizable trends that portend the greatest influence on U. S. security. By being cognizant of such plausible alternatives, American policy makers would have the chance to pursue or avoid them. During the Cold War, American leaders often had little choice but to react to crises. In the more fluid post-Cold War international system, however, the authors believe that the leaders of the world's only superpower can create opportunities both to advance the interests of the United States and preserve the peace of all humankind.

ERVIN J. ROKKE
Lieutenant General, USAF
President, National Defense University

ACKNOWLEDGMENTS

The 2015 Project was begun under the leadership of Colonel Paul Rapalski, USAF, while he was at the Institute for National Strategic Studies. He was instrumental in the most difficult stage—deciding how to approach our investigation of the future security environment: what topics to consider and what methods to use. Any shortcomings in the final product are due to our inability to maintain the high standards he set. We are also grateful to Captain Michael Martus, USN, who saw the project through to its completion; and the officers and academics who contributed to this project by preparing background papers on specific topics, participating in two workshops (one on alliances and one on the environment), making time in their busy schedules to discuss issues with us, or reading earlier drafts. Without their input, this publication would be much the poorer.

PROLOGUE

Evolutionary developments are relatively easy to forecast, but the course of revolutionary events is inherently unpredictable. We live in the midst of a still-unfolding revolution in international relations. It began with the unexpected collapse of the Soviet Empire and the huge increase in East Asian economic strength in the 1980s. This revolution is virtually certain to continue for decades, as the relations among countries are realigned based on their new ratios of strength and weakness.

As is the case with any revolution, the ways in which this upheaval will rearrange the shape of the world cannot be foretold in detail, but educated guesses about the near-term future can be made, using the building blocks with which people construct history. History offers many patterns, but the patterns are based on the same pieces rearranged in different designs. In terms of the history of diplomacy, world economics and war, the essential pieces have been countries, their populations, and their governments. With sufficient knowledge of the ways in which states, peoples and leaders interact, we can determine possibilities and probabilities about how they will operate. This will not produce prophecy but it will suggest the more likely alternatives for the future.

A new factor has entered history in recent decades: accelerated technological change. Technology has influenced history for millennia, but the speed with which technology has been transforming our social and physical environment has accelerated since the advent of the industrial revolution two centuries ago. Recently, it has become obvious that the rate at which technology is transforming our lives is ever faster, with increasingly unpredictable implications for the future.

One result is that the pace of economic development in countries able to take advantage of new technologies has reached astonishing velocity by historical standards. This means that the relationships among states can alter very quickly, with destabilizing results of unprecedented proportions; it is very difficult psychologically to adapt to ever-more-rapid contemporary transformations. Even at the greatly quickened pace brought on by industrialization, it took the United States and Prussia-Germany nearly a century to reach peer status with Britain. Russian industrialization, initiated much later in the 19th century, brought Russia up to roughly the level of Britain in approximately half a century. At the end of the 20th century, we may witness China perform the same feat in relation to the United States in only 25 years or so.

Likewise, the rate of relative decline has increased, because of the same set of factors. Consider the slow decline of Spain vis-a-vis France and Britain in the 17th and 18th centuries, and compare this to the change in British power since the end of the Second World War. Clearly, properly utilized technology, harnessed to wise economic policies, can make an enormous difference in the development rates of two countries beginning at the same level. One celebrated case is that of Ghana and South Korea in the mid-1950s. At the time, the two countries presented an astonishingly similar economic and demographic profile; 35 years later, South Korea has left Ghana far behind.

The leadership of the U.S. Armed Forces is well aware of how technology has transformed the pace of military operations. As the Gulf War illustrated, the rapid communication of complete, accurate information and equally rapid decisionmaking and transmission of orders have become crucial for victory on the battlefield. But this is just a small example of a global phenomenon taking place on a far greater scale that will determine the rise or fall of entire nations. Decisions made at the national level today can have far-reaching consequences for a country's fate in a very short period of time.

Modern history essentially has been determined by sovereign states and by the relations among such states. In fact, the history of our age largely has been the story of the struggle for power within and between states. One way to appreciate this is to consider the extent to which the contemporary person's life is devoted to the creation and acquisition of wealth. At every social level and in almost every place, wealth is being produced in unprecedented amounts compared to previous times. Then consider the proportion of individual wealth that is taxed by the state and spent as the state sees fit. This wealth, when coupled with the modern bureaucratic system and technologies developed since the industrial revolution, has given well-organized states enormous power over their citizens. More important for our purposes, it also has given the large and wealthy states enormous power over the small and poor states. As a result, the very largest and richest states, known as great powers, have been the primary forces shaping recent history.

From time to time, however, a great power has behaved in completely unexpected ways, generally because its population has been swept by an inspiring ideology or directed by an extraordinary leaders. France under Napoleon or Germany under Hitler present examples. Such occurrences are beyond anyone's ability to predict, but in the next several decades, if a charismatic genius were to gain control over one of the great powers while its population was mobilized by some overpowering idea, the consequences for the world either could be catastrophic or marvelous. Such events are rare, but in considering the range of likely possibilities for the great powers outlined below, such an unlikely eventuality should not be dismissed. History is filled with surprises.

I. A WORLD OF GREAT POWERS

Brian R. Sullivan is a social science analyst for the Institute for National Strategic Studies, National Defense University. Previously he taught military history at Yale University and strategy at the Naval War College. He is the co-author of *Il Duce's Other Woman* (William Morrow, 1993) and numerous articles on Italian military, naval, diplomatic, and colonial history. Dr. Sullivan received his Ph.D. in modern European history from Columbia University.

1. THE WORLD OF 2015

In 20 years, the international system will be dominated by a group of great powers. Depending on circumstances, these may number as few as two or three, or as many as five or six. In any case, the United States will remain the greatest, but its supremacy may be challenged by one or more great powers, most likely to be Japan, Russia, India, and China. There may well be a nonstate great power of a different nature: a European Confederation. Alternatively, if the European Union fails to achieve confederal status, a renationalized Germany might emerge as the mightiest state in Europe, although perhaps not quite enjoying the status of a great power. Finally, two other countries may be approaching great-power status in the year 2015: Indonesia and Brazil. But even under optimum conditions, neither likely could achieve true great-power status before the third decade of the 21st century, and probably not until a decade or two later.

THE INTERNATIONAL SYSTEM

One way to consider the possibilities for the world in which these states will interact is to reject the validity of some recent theories about the direction in which the international system is evolving. Contrary to one of those theories, history will not come to an end.[1] Human nature scarcely has been altered by the resolution of the Cold War, and the age-old struggle among states over power and wealth will continue. Nor is it especially likely that wars over the next 20 years will be caused by a clash of civilizations.[2] Conflicts between countries do not arise primarily from differences in religion or culture, nor are alliances generally built on such foundations. This is not to deny the great importance of religion or culture in shaping history, but, as the next chapter will elaborate, enmities or coalitions between states form, above all, on the basis of state interest (raison d'état), not value systems. Consider how racist Nazi Germany allied with Japan in World War II, or how the atheistic, Communist Soviet Union allied with democratic, capitalist Britain and the United States in that same conflict. Future alliances and wars could easily present the same peculiar combinations.

A third popular theory suggests that the spread of democracy to all the great powers would prevent war.[3] To be sure, democracy possibly may spread to all the great powers by 2015, but if it does, it will not preclude war among them. Democracy will no more necessarily prevent international rivalry among free states than it has prevented domestic struggles for power and wealth within democratic polities. So long as democratic states possess armed forces, if friction between two grows severe enough, it could lead to interstate violence. Young democracies seem particularly prone to war, as was the United States in the first half of the 19th century. Unlike an internal democratic system, the international system as we know it, even constructed entirely from democracies, will not always resolve major interstate disputes peacefully.

Finally, it is unlikely that the world will divide into two opposing camps based on wealth: a rich North and a poor South.[4] The weak states, even if they could overcome their myriad differences and unite against the strong, would be no match for them. Instead, in the future as before, the strong states will do largely as they wish; the weak states mostly will be forced to accommodate themselves to the balance of power.

EUROPEAN ANALOGY

Another way to envision the world of 2015 is to conceive of it as similar to the European system of 1648 to 1945, but projected on a global scale. During those three centuries, Europe contained a number of great powers that used their superior military might and riches to divide most of the world among them as colonial empires or spheres of influence. These European countries engaged in ceaseless struggle and periodic war in an attempt by each to increase its power at the expense of the others. Although concentrated in Europe, these conflicts were waged outside of that continent as well, to the dismay of non-Europeans helpless to protect themselves. Eventually, two non-European countries gained the tools necessary to become great powers: the United States and Japan; initially in self-defense, they joined the great-power struggle.

After World War II, when European and Japanese power collapsed, the resulting global vacuum was filled for a time by the United States and the Soviet Union. During the Cold War, Europe and Japan recovered, while a number of new non-European countries acquired the technology and wealth to make dramatic increases in their power. The disintegration of the U.S.S.R. and American unwillingness to exercise world hegemony has created something of a new vacuum. This will be filled partly by the handful of great powers that have emerged or re-emerged during the final decades of the present century or that will do so in the first few decades of the 21st century. The new set of great powers will no longer be crowded in upon each other on the same continent as before. Technology will give each of them at least a hemispheric military reach over the next two decades, and their interests will conflict just as sharply as those of the Europeans once did. In other words, the history of the world for at least the next half century will flow logically out of and be a larger projection of European history since the mid-17th century.

But while the world of 2015 may witness great-power rivalry on a global scale, rather than merely on a continental scale, such a struggle likely would focus on Asia. Four of the potential great or near-great powers—India, China, Japan and Indonesia—will be Asian states and a fifth—Russia—is likely to still retain extensive Asian territories in 20 years. India, China and Russia are all in potential danger of fragmentation. Yet, alternatively, China and Russia could remain united, grow greatly in strength and embark on aggressive foreign policies 15 to 20 years from now. Furthermore, Indonesia, currently of rather negligible strength, may enjoy a great surge of power over the next three to four decades.

THE RISE AND FALL OF GREAT POWERS

Few other events so destabilize the international order as the appearance or disappearance of a great power. Therefore, with its concentration of five great powers on a single continent and the possibility that some of them may rise or fall precipitously, Asia presents the most likely locale for great power clashes in the 2015 period.

The world of the global great powers will present other mixtures of the new along with the familiar. The sovereign state, the foundation of the old international system, will remain strong in most regions of the world. In fact, the authority of governments of functioning states—a monopoly on armed force, the power to exploit a country's wealth, the ability to mobilize people, control over telecommunications—will in many ways increase because technological advances will enlarge the scope of these powers. For example, recent and forthcoming advances in communications technology will spread information faster and farther; the spread of information generates ideas; the spread of scientific ideas generates their practical application in new technologies; new technologies generate wealth. In areas where conditions are favorable, notably East Asia, this generation of wealth is resulting in economic growth at historically unprecedented rates. Governments that efficiently exploit such wealth can convert it into ever-greater power. Thus, the great powers, richest of all states, will enjoy immense economic and military might.

The most concentrated form of state power is well-armed military force. The most powerful arms are nuclear weapons. As nuclear and missile technologies become more accessible and an increasing number of states acquire high levels of wealth, the proliferation of nuclear weapons is sure to increase the number of nuclear powers. By 2015, 20 to 30 countries may possess nuclear arsenals. However, nuclear proliferation will severely limit their freedom to wage war. This will be perhaps the most significant change in the international system 20 years hence.

When midranking and even small states (not to be confused with weak, poor states) possess nuclear arms, the use of military power, even by great powers against small powers, will be severely circumscribed. Throughout history, great powers have had the ability to wage total war (the destruction of an opponent's armed forces, the occupation of its territory, the subjugation of an enemy to one's will). Such war could be waged between great powers and, even more easily, by great powers against lesser powers. After the Soviet Union acquired nuclear weapons, however, it quickly ceased to be practical for the United States and the U.S.S.R. to consider waging total war against each other. As the nuclear arsenals of the two countries grew, it became problematical for either to wage total war even against a weak ally of the other. But nuclear proliferation will extend this logic to an ever-increasing number of states by 2015. A great power will find it dangerous to wage anything other than limited war against even the least well-armed small state possessing nuclear weapons. This transformation of warfare, the worldwide extension of developments that began in 1945, may prove far more influential by 2015 than during any ongoing revolution in military affairs (e.g., in information-based warfare or long-range precision strike).

However, it can be anticipated that the great powers will not accept with resignation such severe limits on their ability to use force. By their very nature, states seek to preserve and expand their power, their spheres of influence and their autonomy of action. To have great military strength but to be unable to exercise it, even in the form of threat, is too contradictory a condition for a state government to endure. In consequence, given the great amounts of wealth that they will control and the ever-expanding capabilities of technology, the major states will undoubtedly fund programs both to devise defenses against nuclear weapons and to develop new means to wage total war. Whether or not such programs produce concrete results over the next quarter century will be a major determinant of the nature of the international system of that period.

2. A EUROPEAN CONFEDERATION

In 2015, the European *Union* likely will have developed into a European *Confederation,* although a relatively weak one. After nearly 40 years of strengthening, the ties binding the members of the EU have become so firm that there is a rather small chance of the union being broken over the next 20 years. By 2015, European economic unification likely will be more advanced than political or military cohesion. Nonetheless, even the latter areas of European integration probably will be considerably more advanced than at present. For one thing, continued European economic unification, as well as cost pressures, will stimulate mergers among national defense corporations, fostering security and defense policy unification as an inevitable result. But if Europe were to come under a serious sustained threat, particularly from across the Mediterranean or from Russia, it is possible that the process of European defense and political unification could accelerate.

The European Confederation of 2015 may consist of about 25 countries[5] with the membership of another 10[6] or so pending. A firm Franco-German alliance may form the nucleus of the group. Based on that foundation, the center of the Confederation would be made up of a fully integrated core group of another four to eight states that could be rightly described as a European Federation. Around this federation would be two or three rings of other states in different stages of integration with the core group.

The Federation probably would be no firmer than the United States was before 1861 and probably less so. The larger Confederation probably would be unified no closer than the United States was under the Articles of Confederation. After centuries of history as sovereign states, the members of the European Confederation will find it difficult to surrender their independence to a higher authority, but the range of integration of the member states would be far wider than the two alternatives of statehood or territorial status familiar to Americans.

As American expansion westward altered the relations among the regions of the United States, so will the enlargement of the European Union (EU) to the east. German influence will grow now that the Twelve have become the Fifteen. It will increase even more so after the likely addition of Poland, Hungary, the Czech Republic, and Slovenia to the European Union. For that reason, further expansion of the EU probably will involve the same kind of coupled admissions that characterized the expansion of the American Union in the first half of the 19th century. France and its supporters would probably insist on the inclusion of such countries aligned more closely with them, such as Malta, Switzerland, Romania, and possibly Serbia, to balance the admission of states closer to Germany, such as some or all of the Baltic Republics and Croatia.

RELATIONS WITH RUSSIA

As the European Union both advances eastward and increases its internal cohesion, its relations with Russia will assume increasing importance. Latvia, Estonia, Ukraine and Moldova will come under increasing pressure to join either the Confederation or a Russian-dominated bloc. If Russian expansionism revives and pushes westward, it will give major impetus to the formation of a common European security and foreign policy system. In turn, European-Russian friction will force the Confederation to settle any still-outstanding questions about the role and nature of the Western European Union (WEU) and the North Atlantic Treaty Organization (NATO), and the relationship between the two defense organizations.

If a commitment to the defense of Europe is still seen by Americans as in their interest, the Europeans would welcome a revitalization of NATO as the best possible guarantee of transatlantic cooperation against an expansionist Russia. But NATO would probably be redrawn as a bilateral alliance (possibly trilateral, if Canadian unity survives) between the United States and the European Union. The WEU might replace NATO as the security link among the European states, absorbing the Partnership for Peace as well. (It is difficult to imagine that the European Confederation or the Russians would long tolerate a distinct American military role in areas likely to be divided between them in one manner or another.)

Russian membership in the European Union anytime in the next 20 or even 30 years seems fairly unlikely, although not totally impossible. This is not to rule out an eventual European Federation stretching from the Azores to the Bering Strait, but such a development almost certainly lies beyond the period of this report. On the other hand, the economic ties between Russia and the European Union will probably grow much closer over the coming two decades, even if relations between the two are tense. Without exaggeration, one might compare the socioeconomic and political relationship of the Europeans to the Russians over the next century to that of Rome to western Europe in the period 100 B.C. to A.D. 300, or to that of the Christian missionaries to northern and eastern Europe in the early-Medieval period.

THE SOUTHERN PERIPHERY

A second, although lesser, potential threat to European security may lie to the south and southeast: North Africa, the Balkans, and the Middle East. If convulsed by war, revolution, religious extremism or economic chaos, these regions would pose fewer concrete challenges to the defense of Europe on military lines than would an expansionist Russia. They might, however, present a more serious political threat to the unification of Europe and to the maintenance of transatlantic ties. A renewed Russian threat would tend to unite Europe and probably bring a reinvigorated American commitment to European security. The Scandinavian and Germanic states are far less sensitive to troubles in the Mediterranean region than the European countries on the northern edge of that sea.

Americans would almost certainly react far more strongly to a Russian merger with Belarus or to a Russian-Ukrainian crisis than to a wave of Arab refugees flooding into Spain, France, and Italy. The failure of the northern Europeans or Americans to offer sufficient assistance in the latter case to the southern Europeans could place the EU, NATO or both under immense strain.

Sub-Saharan Africa may also present a locale for friction between the Europeans and other great powers. Not only France but Britain, Belgium, Portugal, Spain and Italy retain a range of ties to their former African colonies. A European Confederation would also be the closest great power to Africa, particularly sensitive to the security of its trade routes through the Strait of Gibraltar, the Mediterranean, the Suez Canal and the Red Sea. But French ties to Francophone Africa are the most important of these and could well determine the general nature of relations between the European Union and Black Africa. As partial compensation for the increase of German influence in a European Confederation, the French will probably receive a general Confederation commitment to the defense of their interests in Africa. If African states collapse in increasing numbers, such a relationship might involve no more than a leading European role in humanitarian assistance missions. Africa will remain a great depository of resources, regardless of the political and economic status of its inhabitants, and not all African states are necessarily doomed to a miserable future. Some may develop into attractive markets and trading partners. In either case, if the Europeans come to see Africa as their special preserve, possibly as their sphere of influence, they may clash with other great powers that refuse to recognize such an exclusive relationship.

The Europeans also might attempt to assume a predominant role in the Middle East. During the Cold War, European interests were often at odds with those of both the United States and the Soviet Union in the area, but the divided European states were no match for the United States and the Soviet Union in the struggle for regional influence. A united Europe, however, would be far more evenly balanced with a weakened Russia and a more lightly armed United States and would enjoy the advantage of superior geographic position. Expanded Indian and Chinese needs for oil because of far larger national economies and the requirements of a renationalized Japan for the same petroleum may force a limited Europe to exert other pressures on the Middle East. Such multisided rivalry could produce a variety of coalitions and antagonisms among the great powers, as well as between each of the great powers and the Middle Eastern states themselves.

Whatever aims the Europeans adopt, they will possess significant advantages in pursuit of their goals: rich cultural variety based on centuries of wealth, high levels of education and global experience. The European Confederation of 2015 could consist of two dozen diverse countries engaged in an invigorating process of continental rejuvenation. This wide, creative heterogeneity at the service of unified goals will likely produce some astonishing successes.

In contrast to the other countries discussed in this chapter, Europe's future over the next 20 years seems more certain. Nonetheless, it violates common sense and ignores the unpredictable nature of history to insist that Western and Central Europe will inevitably coalesce into a confederation by 2015 and pull Eastern Europe into its orbit. While unlikely, alternatives to a European Confederation are possible over the next generation. Three alternative futures follow a recapitulation of the most likely future for Europe.

ALTERNATIVES

1. A European Confederation

Apart from unpredictable internally-generated decisions by the West Europeans themselves to decrease or increase the pace of their political integration, possible pressures on Europe from Russia or from across the Mediterranean may hasten the formation of a confederation, in response to one or another such threats.

2. The Disintegration of the European Union

Since the end of the Cold War, both nationalism and regionalism have revived noticeably in a number of the members of the European Union. Among the major members, these tendencies have shown special vigor in Britain, France, Spain, and Italy. Nonetheless, France remains rather firmly linked to Germany, forming the essential core of the EU. While the Franco-German relationship may become strained over the coming decade, it seems likely to endure, eventually to grow stronger yet. But there are some signs that nationalism or regionalism might grow stronger in Britain, Spain, and Italy. Either or both might disrupt or even end the cohesion of the EU.

The economic requirements that the EU will impose on its members as prerequisites for greater European integration might create strains on the different regions of Italy and Spain. Already, major differences divide northern and southern Italy, and Catalonia and the rest of Spain. Similar problems afflict Belgium. If the movement toward a European Confederation added to such tensions, three-way struggles might develop among regions, national governments and the EU. It is not entirely inconceivable that such splits might prompt one or more EU members to abandon membership rather than exacerbate national divisions. On the other hand, certain regions might attempt to break from their country rather than lose the benefits of EU membership. One or more political crises of unpredictable resolutions could result. Such an assault on national prerogatives might disrupt the process of European integration and even cause the disintegration of the EU itself.

National pride or socioeconomic interests might encourage one or more EU members to leave the Union. While remote, the chances for such a movement to capture majority support in Britain cannot be dismissed out of hand. Such a reaction in Britain might also influence one or more Scandinavian countries. The departure of one or more of its members would not necessarily cause the EU to crumble. In fact, the departure of those states less enthusiastic about deeper union might even encourage the remaining states to carry out an even more ambitious program of integration. But the departure of a major EU member might produce a chain reaction, leading to the death of the dream of European unity.

3. A Renationalized Germany

Germany is the major EU member most committed to the movement of Europe toward true federation. But even if the EU remains intact, it is conceivable that the combination of revived nationalism in Britain, France, and Italy might end progress toward deeper union and even reverse recent developments in that direction. Under such circumstances, the ironic result might be to cause a revival of nationalism in Germany.

If friction between the Russians and their neighbors over the next decade were to threaten the Germans, and if the United States were to disengage from Europe at the same time that the EU had halted its evolution toward greater union, the Germans might feel forced to seek other forms of protection. The most likely option might be for the Germans to form a smaller group of protectorates and satellites, mold a security pact among them, rearm and then face the Russians. Such a German-led pact might seek accommodation with Russia or, failing that, might rearm and confront Russia. Ukraine might become the object of intense rivalry between Germany and Russia, or Ukraine could decide to choose sides. Under one or the other circumstances, it is not entirely inconceivable that the Germans might even make the painful decision to acquire weapons of mass destruction as a means of defense.

While unlikely, such developments would completely disrupt whatever European unity remained. In a worst-case scenario, 2015 might even witness a Franco-Russian alliance against Germany and its coalition. Alternatively, France might be coerced into an alliance with Germany, prompting a security pact among Britain, Italy and Russia. In either case, Europe would re-experience the kinds of divisions, suspicions, and dangers it suffered throughout the 18th and 19th centuries.

INDICATORS

❏ *Success or failure to restructure the European Union, 1996–1997.* If the European Union is to progress to confederation, its own institutions need to be strengthened at the expense of the intergovernmental bodies presently directing the Union. The recent admission of three new countries to the Union will make the present system even more unworkable than it already is. Most important would be increased authority for the European Parliament. If these developments occur, movement toward a common European security and foreign policy will follow, along with resolution of the questions regarding the WEU and NATO. Moreover, a central European core of states will form around France and Germany, tugging the rest of the Union behind them. But if nationalist sentiments triumph over Europeanism, the crucial Franco-German bond may begin to weaken. The outcome of the InterGovernmental Conference in 1996 will provide an important indicator of the direction in which the European Union is moving.

❏ *Growth of neo-Fascist parties over the next decade.* Strong neo-Fascist parties would oppose the further integration of the European Union in favor of strong nationalist policies. Such parties would also oppose the diminution of the role of the state in the economy and the reduction of the large social welfare programs necessary to make Europe more competitive with the United States and Japan. The loss of jobs and benefits that will result from such reforms, however, could make neo-Fascist parties very attractive to the victims of such a restructuring of the European economies. A dominant or even strong neo-Fascist movement in one of the major EU members could cause serious friction within the Union and even block its progress toward greater cohesion.

❏ *The appearance of a charismatic leader.* The importance of this factor was stressed before; such a leader would be particularly influential in Europe over the next decade. The people of the European Union lack the exciting set of ideas necessary to mobilize their enthusiasms and lead them toward common goals. The appearance of a charismatic leader devoted to uniting Europe could move the continent toward confederation far more swiftly than otherwise. Likewise, a nationalistic leader of genius, opposed to the unification of Europe, especially if he or she appeared in France or Germany, could severely hamper or even wreck the process of European integration.

❑ *Admission of the "Visegrad States" to the European Union by 2000.* Such an expansion of united Europe eastward is essential to satisfy German security needs and to allow Germany's weak eastern neighbors to enjoy the protection of Europe, not just of Germany. Such a development would also make permanent some of the Russian losses in Europe and buttress the other potential targets of renewed Russian imperialism. It is unlikely, of course, that the Visegrad states could receive the levels of subsidy that the European Community supplied to Portugal, Spain, and Greece, so the admission of Poland, the Czech Republic, Hungary, and even Slovakia to the Union depends on the degree of economic reform and growth they can accomplish over the next 5 years. If these four states are left outside the European Union beyond the turn of the century, German dissatisfaction with the Union will grow and German renationalization may well result.

❑ *Expansion of the European Union to include Baltic and Balkan States around 2010.* Such an increase in Union territorial expanse would decisively tip the balance of power in Europe against the Russians. It would increase the chances for Ukraine to remain independent (although if it survives for the next 15 years, it may well be safe from Russian imperialism in any case). Such expansion might even precede Ukraine joining the Union sometime around 2015. Baltic, Balkan and Ukrainian membership in a European Federation could reduce German influence decisively and create a truly European great power. Such a federation would be more populous, richer and potentially more powerful militarily than the United States. Its existence would even raise the possibility of a Russo-American security alliance as a counterweight or, alternatively, the eventual admission of Russia to the European Federation.

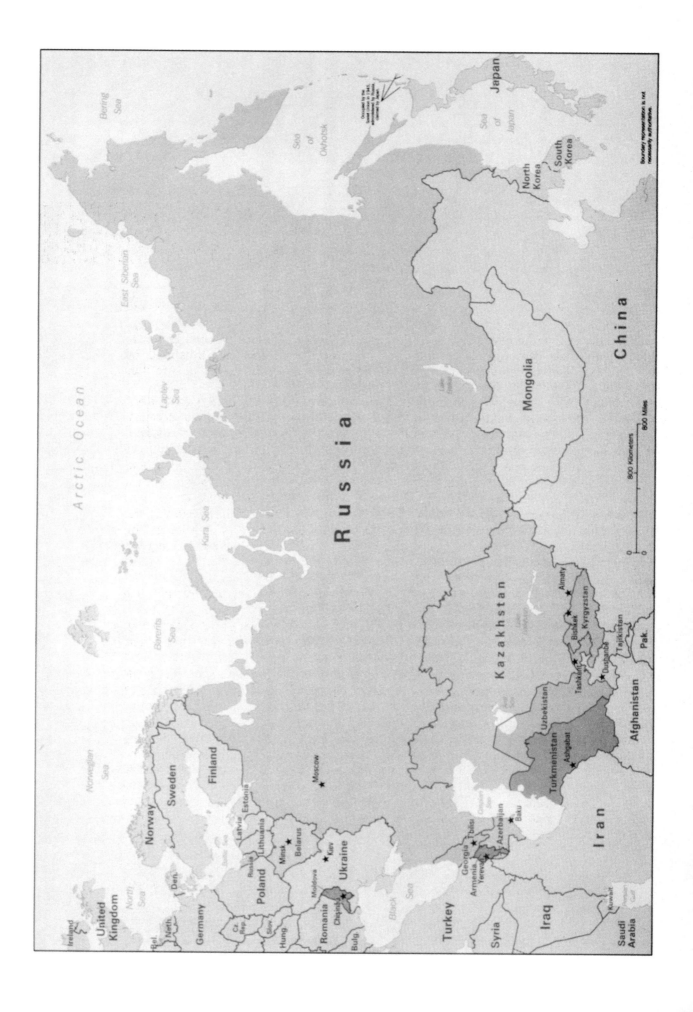

3. RUSSIA

Unlike Europe, the future of which can be envisioned as an evolution toward or away from greater unity, the choices open to Russia are far more revolutionary. In terms of foreign and security policy, the essential question the Russians must answer is whether or not to break with their centuries-old tradition of expansion into territories inhabited by non-Russians. Almost as important, they must determine their national identity. Are they Europeans, Eurasians or uniquely Russians? The various possible answers to the first and second questions are closely linked in their potential influence on the country. The Russians are well aware of their present weakness and its certain continuation for several decades. Thus, even if they choose re-expansion, logically they must focus their ambitions within the confines of the achievable. For example, re-expansion as Russians would suggest Belarus or Kazakhstan as targets, with a need for the best possible relations with China and Japan to protect Siberia and the Russian Far East. The consequences of such a Russia for Europe have been referred to above. On the other hand, a Russian sense of solidarity with Europe, a rejection of irredentism and a concentration on developing the huge resources within Russia's present borders would lead to good relations with the former Soviet republics and lay the foundation for eventual Russian admission to a European Federation, although well beyond 2015.

Without an additional national catastrophe to persuade them otherwise, the Russians will continue to think of themselves as an exceptional people; in that, they are not much different from Americans, Indians, Chinese or Japanese. This Russian national feeling, however, is linked to their history of heavy reliance on military force to express their sense of superiority. This tradition suggests that they will be sorely tempted to retake at least some of their recent territorial losses. In a few months in 1991, the Russians lost lands conquered slowly over three centuries and paid for with incalculable suffering, the loss of tens of millions of Russian lives and huge amounts of treasure. To expect the Russians to accept the loss of what they had bought so dearly and in which they had invested so much of their sense of national pride, is to ask a great deal. One can argue that the Germans came to accept a similar defeat after 1945, but Germany had been ground into rubble by the time World War II ended and then was divided and occupied for decades. This debacle had a permanent and largely beneficial influence on the German national psyche. The Russian Empire, on the other hand, has slipped away as if in a dream, and most Russians do not have the vaguest understanding of how it happened, nor are they reconciled to the fact.

Still, economic reality has made it clear to most Russian citizens and leaders alike, that their country is in no condition to initiate wars of conquest any time soon. The wreckage caused by 70 years of Soviet economic mismanagement, environmental pillage and mass murder is impossible to calculate. As a comparison, the eastern German states are going to need $1.5 to 2 trillion over 15 to 20 years to be brought up to the level of western Germany. By extrapolation, it would require all the investment capital of the entire human race, spent over a generation on Russia alone, to raise it to the economic level of Western Europe. Obviously, no such miracle is going to happen, and Russia is going to remain backward compared to Western Europe for a long time to come. One can assume that it would take until about 2035 at the very soonest, with the consistent application of sound economic policy, for the average Russian to enjoy a standard of living approaching that of the typical Western European or Japanese.

In the shorter run, over the next 20 years Russia's need to concentrate on internal development will likely give its larger neighbors a respite from any possible Russian revival of expansionism. (However, some of Russia's smaller neighbors may suffer the fate of the Chechens.) This period will also be crucial for the creation of new Russian political structures and for giving the Russian people an opportunity for reflection and debate about their national purpose. For all the heavy pressures that culture and geography inflict on the Russian soul, they still face a range of genuine choices. Furthermore, thanks to the collapse of totalitarianism and to the development of new communications technologies, Russians enjoy far better access to the outside world (and the outside to them) than ever before in history. Thus, Russians will have the opportunity to make informed decisions about their future. Despite their past, tragedy is not inevitable for the Russians. Let us consider what appear to be their realistic alternatives by 2015, beginning with a bleak one.

ALTERNATIVES

1. Declining Russia

The Russian Federation may decay, because of failure of economic reform, strong regional tendencies, the strength of organized crime, and the success of local cliques to ignore instructions from the central government. The military might remain relatively powerful politically as an autonomous force but decline technologically because of a lack of funding. Some areas, such as St. Petersburg, the Black Sea coast, and Vladivostok might enjoy prosperity; others, including Central Russia and the Urals might decline into penury. These regions would still be tied to Moscow by vague nationalist sentiments, howerver. Areas like Tatarstan, Yakutia and the Far East might attain a highly-autonomous status because of local ethnicity, wealth or the lure of powerful neighbors on the other side of Russia's borders. Moscow would possess little power in a country with a weak overall economy, high unemployment, wretched social welfare programs, low levels of public health, powerful criminal gangs, and loyalties tied to communal and local authorities.

Such a Russia would pose a threat to Eurasian stability not as predator but as prey. This Russia would be a haven for international organized crime. It might sell its U.N. Security Council veto to the highest bidder. China might attempt to regain the Russian Far East, lost in the 19th century through the so-called "Unequal Treaties." Alternatively, if China also fell victim to regionalism, a new state in the Far East might emerge composed of both former Chinese and Russian territories. Such a new country might turn to Japan for aid and bring back Japanese influence to the Asian mainland, as in the period 1905 to 1945.

Of course, such a Russia would pose no threat of reconquest to the former Soviet Republics. Those in Europe would naturally gravitate toward the European Confederation and be well along the road to membership by 2015. The Russian armed forces would be incapable of significant power projection abroad. They would probably be based on a small, all-volunteer army to protect the heartland, serve as a Praetorian Guard for the central government and beat down the weaker secessionist movements. The autonomous regions would create their own militaries in the guise of territorial militias. While small, such forces in the richer regions might be quite capable.

The strategic nuclear forces would likely decline because of Moscow's inability to fund new military technologies. Still, over the next 20 years, Russia would continue to possess enough nuclear weapons to wreak havoc on other great powers. Given Russian poverty, the temptation for either the state or individuals to sell nuclear weapons to others would be great. This danger might make "Declining Russia" a major threat to world peace.

2. The United States of Eurasia

Russia might begin to decline as described above but be saved from such degradation along the way. Moscow might be able to reassert some of its authority under a charismatic leader or movement, especially if Russians felt threatened by China. Nonetheless, many of the problems previously mentioned would limit the central government's options. Moscow would be less able to force the regions into submission than to negotiate a new political arrangement. Russian officials might propose the creation of a Eurasian counterpart to the European Confederation.

Such an appeal might be extended to some of the former Soviet Republics as well. Pragmatic and sentimental arguments might be combined. The economic structures of the tsarist empire and the Soviet Union still connect such countries and could be rebuilt along healthy lines. If the Russian economy enjoys stronger growth than the other ex-Soviet republics, the latter might see many benefits in linking their economies to that of Russia even more closely. Moscow would cease to threaten its non-Russian neighbors and the far-flung Russian regions in the context of a true confederal system. A Eurasian confederation could afford to maintain armed forces powerful enough to defend all, unlike the weak forces of several smaller states. Moscow's nuclear umbrella would be extended to the confederation, too. Many ex-Soviet Republics have no real sense of nationalism and are riven internally by ethnic differences—but they do have a history of union within the Russian Empire dating back a century or more. Membership in a United States of Eurasia could be attractive for these reasons. In contrast, membership in a European Confederation of wealthy, culturally Catholic and Protestant powers ultimately might prove ·less appealing for historical reasons to the ex-Soviet states than would a loose union with an economically developing group of poorer but more equal Orthodox and Moslem states.

Beyond 2015, such a confederation might roughly duplicate the history of the United States by transformation into a centralized federation. Under those circumstances, Russian dominance might well reassert itself. But by the mid-twenty-first century, Russia might be bordered on the west by a powerful European Federation and on the east by a mighty Chinese superpower. Under those circumstances, the opportunities that Russia had in the 18th, 19th and 20th centuries for expansion would not exist. In order to expand, Russia would have to ally with one against the other, with potentially terrible consequences for humankind. Or, content with a huge and potentially prosperous federation, the Russians might very well choose peaceful economic competition as the preferable new form of Russian expansion. But these possibilities take us beyond the time frame of this study.

3. A Russian Nation-State

Russia may develop into a democratic and liberal capitalist state, but to do so would require Russia to abandon the legacies of its Tsarist and Soviet past. Such a Russia would probably be organized along federal lines, much like contemporary Germany. This would almost certainly mean a contraction of Russian territory, giving freedom to those who do not feel a sense of Russian nationalism. To include such non-Russians in a new "free Russia" would require forms of coercion incompatible with democracy. Realistically, such a democratic Russia could probably be born only out of a major disaster like a lost war with the Chinese or an unsuccessful intervention into Ukraine. These kinds of serious reversals, such as those suffered by the Axis Powers in World War II, can lead to revisions of identity and national rebirth.

This Russia would no longer be a multiethnic empire but a true national state of overwhelmingly Russian character. It would probably extend no farther than western Siberia and no farther south than the Volgograd region. A national Russia would receive an influx of millions of Russians departing former areas of Russian conquest and would be reconciled to the permanent loss of the Baltics and Ukraine. But such a Russia might very likely include Belarus, with its heavily Russian culture and ethnicity, and even might include the heavily Russian-inhabited areas of northern Kazakhstan.

A reduced Russia would face serious economic and resocialization challenges. By 2015, however, it could enjoy a high level of political and economic stability. Such a Russia might be quite democratic but still suffer from occasional outbreaks of xenophobia and racism. The relatively small non-Russian ethnic minorities even could be treated like second-class citizens, but Russia would possess more defensible borders than at present and would no longer have the problem of large, potentially disloyal non-Russian minorities. On the other hand, the mass migration of Russians out of the northern Caucasus, eastern Ukraine, eastern Siberia, and possibly northern Kazakhstan might destabilize those regions and bring chaos along Russia's new borders. China might penetrate the area of the former Russian Far East. Ukraine and Poland would enjoy positions far closer to equality with Russia than at present. Under these circumstances, Russia would be forced to court Europe and could even move into a European Confederation by 2015, but it would have to address its possible human rights problems and vestiges of hypernationalism in order to qualify for admission.

4. Imperial Russia

The pull of the past may prove too strong for the Russians to escape over the next 20 years. They may abandon their experiment with democracy, rally to an authoritarian government, and renew their ancient attempts to impose their hegemony over Eurasia. The regions and the non-Russians within the revived empire would be subjugated to harsh central rule. Russia would remain capitalist but with large state participation in the economy. This Russia would be, or would approximate, a neo-Fascist state. Nonetheless, it is not inconceivable that such a Russia would restore the monarchy as a powerful symbol of Russian imperialism and divine right to rule over vast territories inhabited by non-Russians.

By 2015, the economy of this Russia would be weak, and Russian technology outmoded. Repression and authoritarianism do not blend well with information-based creativity. Imperial Russia would present an aggressive and bombastic facade to the world. But it would probably be unable to take much effective action to back up its attitudes toward the other great powers; instead, the Russians would put severe pressure on their weaker neighbors. Reincorporation of Belarus would be the priority and the Belarussians might be persuaded to accept a bloodless *Anschluss*. Because of their large Russian populations, Ukraine and Kazakhstan might be invaded and would be at least subjected to Russian-supported terrorism and insurgency. The Transcaucasian and Central Asian republics would be heavily pressured into accepting protectorate status.

Imperial Russia could not be easily contained or appeased by its immediate neighbors. The ideological basis for such a regime virtually would require Russian confrontation with states on their borders. Wars of conquest would be highly attractive to such a state to gain prestige and wealth, and to siphon off unstable and criminal elements dangerous at the center. Russian aggression would be met by ostracism and hostility by the other great powers. This would reinforce deep-seated Russian xenophobia and paranoia, driving the regime even further into imperialism to gain resources and create a military defense in depth.

Imperial Russia would be too weak to engage directly the other great powers over the next 20 years. These Russians would offer the United States and the Europeans recognition of their spheres of influence in return for similar recognition. Imperial Russia would seek agreement to demilitarize at least part of Eastern Europe as a buffer zone between it and the European Confederation. Influenced by racism, historical enmity and geographical proximity, Imperial Russia would view India, China and Japan as rivals and potential victims. While seeking peace with the United States and Europe, it would concentrate it armed forces in Central Asia and the Far East.

This Russia would be able to draw on some strong national traditions and considerable indigenous resources, but it would probably not long survive. By 2015, it would be facing many of the same problems that led to Soviet collapse in the 1980s and for largely the same reasons. Imperial Russia might overplay a weak military hand with China and be crushed in an ensuing war. Even if it escaped military defeat, Imperial Russia would find the costs of empire impossible to sustain for long, especially in a world in which it fell technologically ever more behind. But the leaders of such a state would be unlikely to depart as meekly as Mikhail Gorbachev did. The last Soviet Party Secretary undoubtedly would be held up as a vile example of treason and cowardice. His successors in an Imperial Russia could revert to mass slaughter rather than allow their empire to slip away from them. At some point, such crimes and the anarchy they would unleash would probably force European, Indian and Chinese intervention, with unpredictable and dangerous consequences, but this nightmare would probably not occur until sometime after 2015.

INDICATORS

❏ *The Russian Birthrate.* Demographics will have a crucial influence on the Russian future. Russian births have declined severely for the past decade, and this drop hasbecome more pronounced with each passing year. Recently, Russia has been experiencing an actual decline in population as deaths outnumber births. If this situation continues or grows worse, Russia will lack the population necessary to deal with its economic problems and to create large armed forces. Furthermore, a continuing demographic decline will indicate deep pessimism on the part of the Russian people. If the population begins to grow again, however, it will indicate a return of optimism and more promising signs of the return of Russian power in 20 years' time.

❏ *The Restructuring of the Economy.* It is difficult to imagine that any future Russia would revert to Stalinism; its failure remains blatantly obvious. But if the state does not privatize to a significant degree or, worse, seeks to regain control of more of the economy, this degree of interference in daily life could signal a move toward Imperial Russia. At the other extreme, libertarian policies, placing the economy at the mercy of organized crime and greedy multinational corporations, would pauperize Russia. This would herald Declining Russia.

❏ *The Fate of Democracy.* Prolonged Russian exposure to millenarian and messianic ideologies, whether tsarist or Communist, has made many susceptible to extremist politics. If neo-Fascists or neomonarchists gain major support, this may indicate the arrival of Imperial Russia. Excessive pragmatism would also endanger Russian democracy by justifying "short-term" authoritarian measures to hold the country together or force the regions to pay their fair share of taxes to the center. In the absence of a strong democratic tradition, it is difficult for the Russians to know where to stop such measures. If Boris Yeltsin or his successor were to revert to such methods, Russian democracy would probably be doomed.

❏ *The Influence of Russian History.* The way in which Russian history is interpreted and taught, particularly at the primary and secondary school levels, may be an important indicator of the intentions at the center. A lumping together of Ivan the Terrible, Peter the Great, Alexander Suvorov, Vladimir Ilyich Lenin, Joseph Stalin, and Marshal Georgiy Zhukov as all great heroes of the Russian nation would suggest the arrival of Imperial Russia. This would be particularly true if the crimes of the Soviet period were explained as sad but necessary actions to expand the power of the state. Alternatively, if the Soviet period is damned but the Tsarist era is embraced with a mythologized nostalgia, this would indicate Declining Russia. If local regions begin to rediscover (or invent) histories totally independent of the center, this would be an even stronger indicator of decline. Russian democracy depends on an open and critical assessment of all periods of Russian history, one prepared to acknowledge the virtues and vices of both but enthusiastic about building a third, better national tradition. German and Italian historiography after 1945 provides models of what a democratic Russia needs in its schools.

❏ The Center's Power of Taxation. At present, the center is being deprived by the regions of sufficient tax revenues. If this continues, expect a declining Russia. A complete reversal, in which the center deprives the regions of any taxation power, would indicate the coming of imperial Russia. A democratic Russia would require a consensual deal with the regions on taxation or, better yet, a limited degree of reimposition of central control over taxation, perhaps accompanied by a revenue-sharing plan.

❑ *The Role of the Military.* If civil control of the military is established, especially under a civilian defense minister and with genuine parliamentary scrutiny of the military, the cause of democracy will have been greatly advanced. Other signs of democratization would include reduced defense budgets and new military doctrine that reduce the role of the armed forces in foreign and domestic policy. However, if the military doctrine introduced in 1993 is retained, but the center lacks the will and resources to apply it, this indicates a declining Russia is coming. Finally, if the doctrine is maintained, defense budgets increased, the military restructured for offensive operations and force projection, Imperial Russia is a likelihood.

❑ *The Powers of the Political Police.* The successor agencies to the KGB remain powerful. If they escape significant reform that places strict limits on their powers or are placed beyond effective public and parliamentary scrutiny, this would represent a real danger to democracy. If the Russian presidency retains direct and complete control over the secret police, even in the name of a crackdown on organized crime, this would suggest the advent of Imperial Russia.

❑ *Siberia and the Far East.* If the Far East and, more important, Siberia, experience strong secessionist movements, the reaction of Moscow will provide indicators about Russia's future. A brutal crackdown would suggest an imperial Russia. A passive reaction accompanied by futile verbal protests would suggest a declining Russia. The breaking of ties as a deliberate policy by the center would suggest the emergence of a Russian nation-state.

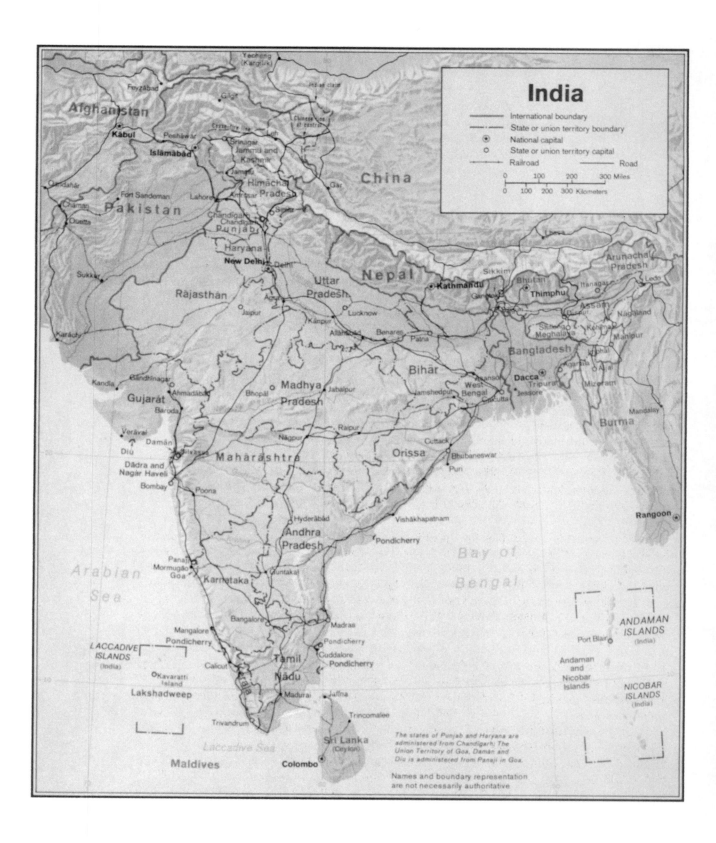

India

- International boundary
- State or union territory boundary
- ⊙ National capital
- ○ State or union territory capital
- ┼┼┼ Railroad
- ─── Road

| 0 | 100 | 200 | 300 Miles |
| 0 | 100 | 200 | 300 Kilometers |

Yecheng (Karghlik)

Feyzâbâd

Afghanistan

Gilgit

Kâbul

Peshâwar

Cease-fire line

Leh

Chinese line of control

Islâmâbâd

Srinagar Jammu and Kashmir

China

Qandahâr

Fort Sandeman

Lahore

Jammu

Himâchal Pradesh

Gar

Chaman

Pakistan

Amritsar

Simla

Lhasa

Quetta

Chandigarh Chandigarh

Punjab

Haryâna

New Delhi   Delhi

Nepal

Arunâchal Pradesh

Sukkur

Sikkim

Ledo

Uttar Pradesh

Kâthmându

Bhutan

Itanagar

Karâchi

Râjasthân

Agra

Lucknow

Gangtok

Thimphu

Assam

Dibrugarh

Nâgâland

Jaipur

Kânpur

Allahâbâd

Benares

Patna

Shillong Meghâlaya

Kohima

Manipur

Bangladesh

Imphâl

Kandla

Gândhinagar

Bihâr

Asansol

West Bengal

Dacca

Tripura

Agartala

Aizawl

Mizoram

Ahmadâbâd

Bhopâl

Madhya Pradesh

Jabalpur

Jamshedpur

Calcutta

Jessore

Gujarât

Baroda

Mandalay

Verâval

Damân

Nâgpur

Raipur

Burma

Diu

Dâdra and Nagar Haveli

Maharashtra

Cuttack

Orissa

Bhubaneswar

Bombay

Poona

Puri

Hyderâbâd

Vishâkhapatnam

Rangoon

Andhra Pradesh

Pondicherry

Bay of Bengal

Panaji

Mormugâo Goa

Karnataka

Guntakal

Arabian Sea

ANDAMAN ISLANDS (India)

Port Blair

Mangalore

Bangalore

Madras

Pondicherry

Andaman and Nicobar Islands

LACCADIVE ISLANDS (India)

Pondicherry

Cuddalore

Pondicherry

Calicut

Tamil Nâdu

Kavaratti Island

NICOBAR ISLANDS (India)

Lakshadweep

Madurai

Jaffna

Trincomalee

Trivandrum

Laccadive Sea

Sri Lanka (Ceylon)

Maldives

Colombo

The states of Punjab and Haryana are administered from Chandigarh. The Union Territory of Goa, Daman and Diu is administered from Panaji in Goa.

Names and boundary representation are not necessarily authoritative.

4. INDIA

Economics and demographics will govern India's success or failure at becoming a great power by 2015. At present, India resembles two countries superimposed on the same territory: a modernizing and rapidly developing middle-class India of some 200 to 300 million and a traditional, impoverished India of some 600 to 700 million. In some ways, the gap between these two groups is widening. From 1950 to 1980, the growth of the Indian Gross National Product (GNP) averaged only 1.4 percent per year, hardly enough to keep up with population growth. From 1980 to 1990, economic growth rates improved, averaging 3.3 percent. But this growth was heavily concentrated in the upper third of the population. The resulting socioeconomic tension is a major cause of both the rise of Hindu extremism and the violent regional separatism which could threaten India's internal stability. The major challenge to overcome, if India is to solve these pressing problems and become a great power, is to close its great social divide by creating a vast Indian lower middle class and industrial working class. India has a relatively short time to raise the standard of living of its poorer citizens before the problem becomes virtually insuperable. With well over half its population under 25, the Indian economy must create hundreds of millions of jobs over the next two decades. Furthermore, the population is rapidly increasing. By 2015, India will have at least 1.2 billion inhabitants.

A closely related difficulty preventing India from becoming a major world power is the heterogeneous nature of its population. India is a subcontinent not only because of its size but also because of the conglomeration of cultures, ethnicities and language groups gathered under the Indian flag. India is the largest piece of the old British Indian Empire, itself largely carved out of the Mogul Empire. As a country descended from two empires, India is not a nation-state, but a third version of the older empires disguised as a democratic federal republic.

The Congress Party, the nationalist organization that gained Indian independence from the British in 1947, tried and failed to maintain the unity of the entire Indian Empire. Instead, independence occurred simultaneously with partition from Pakistan and what would later become Bangladesh. For most of the history of India since then, the republic has been ruled by a Congress Party elite of English-speaking, Western-oriented aristocrats and civil servants. This group vaguely resembles the French-speaking aristocrats who governed Russia in the 18th century—a privileged group alienated culturally from the vast majority of the people they rule. But it has served as the glue binding together the republic's many peoples for the last half-century. Based both on the heritage of Mohandas Karamchand

"Mahatma" Gandhi and on national necessity, the Congress Party stressed toleration and respect for India's large, non-Hindu minorities.

The cosmopolitan Indian ruling class has been reinforced over the past several decades by ties with the Indian diaspora. The English-speaking diaspora of professionals, merchants, and business people is scattered throughout the former British Empire, as well as in Britain itself, the United States, and the Middle East. The diaspora had gone abroad in the days of the British Empire, seeking advantages that poverty-ridden India could not offer. They prospered, thanks to the money they could borrow through family connections at home, hard work, skills, and cultural advantages. But the diaspora was discouraged from returning to India after independence, because of the Soviet-inspired Socialist economic policies of the Congress Party. Beginning in the late 1980s, however, India adopted free-market economics, creating greater opportunities at home. Part of the Western-oriented diaspora has returned to India, bringing back their high level of skills, education, and wealth. Among other accomplishments, they have created a kind of Indian Silicone Valley on the southern plateau of the Bangalore region. The returning diaspora has reinforced and given substance to the Congress Party elite's determination to raise India to great-power status.

However, India has succeeded well enough with its post-independence programs of mass education, autarchic industrialization, public works, agricultural development and expansion of the civil service and armed forces to create a second middle class. This group is heavily concentrated in the Hindi-speaking Hindu population of the northern Ganges Valley. It resents the Congress Party elite for its privileges and envies its power; it has been actively seeking to unseat it for the past few years. Taking advantage of India's democratic politics, some leaders of the Hindi middle class have been using the appeal of extremist Hinduism and Hindi nationalism to appeal to the poor masses of the Ganges Valley. These politicians advocate an exclusivist, Hindi-speaking Hindu India, antagonistic to the tolerant Western cosmopolitanism of the Congress Party elite, to the Indian Moslem, Sikh, and Christian populations of some 150 million and even to the large Tamil-speaking Hindus of the south, the Marathi-speaking Hindus of the west, and the Bengali-speaking Hindus of the northeast. Such divisive national politics threaten to make a bad situation worse. India already is plagued by three separatist insurgencies: by Sikhs in the Punjab, Moslems in Kashmir and various tribes in the northeast each seeking independence. Despite brutal repression by the Indian Army and national police, none of these uprisings has been stifled.

Added to India's internal problems are the closely related foreign problems caused by the collapse of the Soviet Union, the spectacular growth of the Chinese economy, and Pakistan's acquisition of a nuclear weapons capability. Despite some improvement in relations since the Sino-Indian border war in 1962, Indian leaders continue to view China as a grave, long-term threat to Indian security and to Indian aspirations to supremacy in South Asia. India's adoption of free-market economics has improved the growth of its GNP to about 4 percent per annum over the past few years, but this hardly matches China's recent economic growth rate, which averaged 9.4 percent during the 1980s and hovered at about 12 percent during 1992, 1993, 1994, and 1995. Indian leaders are well aware that if these disparities in growth rates continue, Chinese power will dominate all South Asia within a decade. Caught between China's allies to the west and east (Pakistan and Burma) with China firmly in control of Tibet, India could be forced into quasi-vassalage.

Between the mid-1960s and 1991, India counterbalanced China and Pakistan by alliance with the Soviet Union (from which it received both cheap arms and cheap oil) and greatly strengthened itself militarily with successful nuclear weapons, ballistic missiles and satellite programs. But the disintegration of the USSR and the development of Pakistan's own nuclear capability have deprived India of its previous advantages. India can only rely on itself, particularly on the potential of a powerful economy, to reverse its decline relative to China.

❑ India's internal and external difficulties can appear so daunting that the idea of India advancing to great-power status in 20 years' time may seem preposterous. India does possess, however, advantages that could lead to a great surge in its power:

❑ The country has hundreds of millions of relatively well-educated citizens fluent in English. It also possesses a fine English-language university system that for decades has been educating excellent scientists, engineers and technicians. In an age of information-based technology, such widespread access to the world's primary commercial and scientific language gives India a huge advantage over China.

❑ Through the centuries, Indians have displayed a remarkable degree of entrepreneurial skill and financial acumen. While the Socialist economy of the 1947-1991 period inhibited Indian economic growth, it never snuffed out the age-old Indian capitalist tradition.

❑ The Indian state already has in place the tax system, the banking and lending networks, the commercial statutes and business structures necessary for the smooth running of a capitalist economy.

❑ Finally, India has huge numbers of small and large business owners, managers, accountants, financiers, and lawyers prepared and eager to take full advantage of a free market, giving India another great superiority to China.

If India realizes its economic potential, it will produce the technology base and tax revenues necessary to make it a first-class military power. The Indian armed forces already possess excellent traditions, pride and discipline. Properly funded and armed, such forces could draw upon a huge mass of manpower to make India the supreme power in the Indian Ocean region. All this will depend on the choices the Indians make between now and 2015.

ALTERNATIVES

1. Divided India

India may fail to develop its economic potential sufficiently and fall victim to overpopulation. Certain Indian regions, primarily those between Bombay and Bangalore,might become quite prosperous and secede to enjoy their wealth in isolation. Overwhelmed by massive national poverty, the central government might collapse and the country fragment into several states based on local language and religion. For example, the Punjab might emerge as an independent Khalistan closely aligned with Pakistan; Kashmir might unite with Pakistan; Hindu Bengal might merge with Bangladesh; and the

Tamils might declare independence and seize the Tamil-inhabited region of Sri Lanka. However, the Indian Army might manage to keep the country united within a weak confederal structure. Foreign enemies might be kept at bay by a nuclear-armed Indian Air Force still loyal to the center.

Of course, without sufficient revenue, it would prove impossible for the army to remain strong enough to keep such an India united, and the air force could not long maintain its nuclear arsenal. India might struggle on as a confederation by consent of the regions or fragment completely sometime after 2015. In any case, under such conditions, it could not be counted among the great powers.

2. Hindu India

Hindi-speaking Hindus number only about 30 percent of the population. So long as India remains a democracy, such a group cannot gain control of the government. But if Hindu nationalism swept the Marathis, Bengalis, Tamils, Gujaratis, Sindhis, and other language groups of Hindu religion, Indians could elect an intolerant authoritarian government ruled by Hindu extremists. Under such circumstances, large numbers of the cosmopolitan upper classes might flee and the Western-oriented diaspora cease returning to India. The fate of the Moslems would be truly miserable, judged by recent attacks by Hindu mobs on mosques and Moslem neighborhoods in Indian cities. Some would be massacred, some would flee to Pakistan, and the rest would be reduced to servitude. However, such an India could still emerge as a great power, if it pursued economic policies that encouraged high rates of growth.

A Hindu India would likely be a highly bellicose, nationalistic state motivated by a form of Fascist ideology. This India would attempt to crush the insurgencies in the Punjab and Kashmir with unrestrained brutality. It would spend heavily on arms, especially on weapons of mass destruction, to overawe Pakistan and to deter China. Such a government would lay claim to the Indian Ocean as a *mare nostrum*. It would call for American withdrawal from Diego Garcia and demand recognition of the Indian Ocean and its littoral as an Indian sphere of influence. It might use the Tamil-Sinhalese conflict in Sri Lanka as an excuse for military intervention in the island. It would try to pressure Bangladesh into becoming an Indian dependency.

This India would demand a permanent seat on the United Nations Security Council as its due. However, its belligerent behavior would make China and the Western powers opposed to such membership. Depending on Russian reaction, such an Indian bid could disrupt the United Nations indefinitely until the matter were settled.

A Hindu India might provoke war with Pakistan, perhaps unintentionally. But assuming a small but growing Pakistani nuclear arsenal, it seems more likely that India would try to use its growing economic and military power to pull Pakistan into its orbit as a protectorate. Depending on international rivalries, such an India might try to barter its neutrality or military support to America or China. In return, it might demand the abandonment of Pakistan to Indian conquest. Such an India would probably seek a strategic alliance with Russia, as well.

A Hindu India would probably be hostile to Iran, particularly if it allied with China, supported Pakistan, and aided the extremists in Afghanistan and the insurgents in

Kashmir. If Iran were seen as a significant threat in New Delhi, Hindu India would probably react by investing in a major naval building program and strengthening any strategic alliance with Russia to subdue the Central Asian republics, Iran, Pakistan and Afghanistan. In such circumstances, Turkey could be forced to ally with China, Iran, and Pakistan.

Hindu India might seek expansion in East Africa. Uganda, Kenya and Tanzania were used by the British as colonies for the settlement of excess population from the Subcontinent; this policy came to an end with Indian independence, but large ethnic Indian populations remain in the region. If AIDS and new epidemics were to sweep through East Africa and depopulate the area, the ethnic Indians might survive, thanks to their higher standard of living and superior access to health care. An aggressive Hindu India might take advantage of the ensuing opportunity to intervene to "restore order" or provide "humanitarian assistance," only to remain as a *de facto* neocolonial occupier. Such policies would undoubtedly result in serious friction with South Africa and the Arab states.

However, if the Chinese threat grew severe enough, a Hindu India would be forced to abandon such imperialism, soften its anti-Islamic policies and seek a grand alliance with Indonesia, the smaller states of Southeast Asia, Japan, and Russia to contain Chinese expansion. Depending on the degree to which China was threatening its neighbors, such an anti-Sinitic alliance might seek ties with the United States.

3. Democratic India

An economically successful India that rejected Hindu extremism might nonetheless adopt many of the policies described for a Hindu India, but such an India would pursue these policies in a less confrontational and more diplomatic manner. Such an India would stress its democratic ideals as one of the bases for an anti-Chinese understanding with the United States and Japan, should a powerful China disturb the tranquility of Asia. However, even if China were to develop into a peaceful democracy, Chinese-Indian rivalry would continue, even if pursued primarily along economic and political lines.

A strong but democratic India would still display unease with an American naval presence in the Indian Ocean. Depending on the degree of Indian and Chinese dependence on Middle East oil, such an India would seek to be the master of the sea lines of communication in the Indian Ocean. Democratic India would press the argument on the United States that it was a reasonable and peace-loving state that could be trusted to protect American interests in the ocean and to help the United States bear the heavy burden of safeguarding world peace. Democratic India would seek and likely receive a permanent seat on the U.N. Security Council. It would participate enthusiastically in peacekeeping operations both to expand its international influence and to gain favor with American public opinion.

Democratic India would still seek to dominate its region and the Indian Ocean, but it would do so primarily by economic and diplomatic means and through cultural ties to the numerous Indian ethnic communities scattered throughout Africa, the Middle East and Southeast Asia. Democratic India might seek special links to South Africa and Australia. It could stress its sincere desire for tranquility in the Indian Ocean, the powerful tool it possessed in the Indian navy and its interest in security cooperation with the other democracies that lie at the two extreme ends of the ocean.

Even a democratic India sincerely devoted to peace in South Asia might still pursue policies aimed at the effective destruction of Pakistan. Indians of every religion and region are united over the necessity to retain control of Kashmir. They view Pakistan's very existence, and certainly Islamabad's aid to the Kashmiri insurgents, as a threat to Indian unity. If India were to lose a substantial number of its Moslem citizens, it might encourage other Islamic separatist movements in India and also strengthen the appeal of Hindu extremists.

But a democratic India might seek to overwhelm Pakistan by kindness, instead of by force of arms. Over a period of decades, India might seek to alleviate the basic causes of Indo-Pakistani hostility, to stress the common cultural and political origins of the two states, to promote the Western-oriented views of Pakistan's English-speaking elite and to encourage bilateral trade and technological cooperation. A similar Indian effort might be aimed at Bangladesh. While hardly certain and certainly slow, in any case, by 2015, some movement toward the creation of a confederation eventually linking the three states might be perceived.

INDICATORS

What indicators can be listed of the directions in which India might move over the next 20 years? The following should provide some solid clues.

❑ *Immigration and emigration patterns.* The permanent departure of large numbers of well-educated Indians would signify a loss of hope about the economy and/or fears of a rise of religious and regional strife. The return to India of large numbers of the ethnic Indian elite would suggest the opposite.

❑ *The price and availability of oil.* The growth of the Indian economy will depend a great deal on world oil prices and on discoveries of offshore Indian oil fields. Cheap, abundant oil will help India become a great power. Without that, the Indian economy could falter or even collapse.

❑ *Attitudes toward nuclear and missile proliferation.* The degree to which India agrees or refuses to cooperate with efforts to stop the spread of weapons of mass destruction will indicate its degree of suspicion and hostility toward the United States. Indian reaction to an American offer to adhere formally or informally to the nuclear Non-Proliferation Treaty (NPT) and the Missile Technology Control Regime (MTCR) in return for American technical assistance in such matters would be highly revealing.

❑ *Armaments programs and foreign sources of arms.* Since independence, India has begun a number of ambitious, indigenous arms programs, only to repeatedly fail or fall far short of goals. Recently, taking advantage of the return of many Western-educated scientists and technologists, India has initiated a series of expensive ventures with military applications. These include research and development of computers, robotics, fiber optics, radar, microwave applications, superconductivity, composite materials, air-breathing propulsion, stealth technologies and sensors. A monitoring of the progress of these programs will give a good indication of how powerful the Indian military might be in 20 years.

❑ *Indo-Pakistani contacts on their nuclear arsenals, employment doctrine, and safeguards.* Indian willingness to conduct negotiations with Pakistan with regard to their nuclear weapons and their doctrine for employment would be a good omen that India sincerely wished to avoid war and develop cooperative relations with Pakistan.

❑ *The status of Moslems and Sikhs.* An early sign of the rise to power of Hindu nationalism would be widespread persecution of adherents to India's major non-Hindu religions. The government might try to prevent such attacks. But if they continued despite police protection of the minorities, it could signify a Hindu nationalist victory at the polls sometime thereafter.

❑ *Renewal of the Indo-Russian strategic relationship.* India and Russia could rebuild their alliance in a defensive or offensive manner. In the face of Chinese threats, such an alliance might be in America's interest. But if the coalition were to be recreated in a period of Chinese weakness or benevolent international behavior, it could signify Indian and Russian plans for expansion and aggression.

❑ *Policies toward states adjacent the Indian Ocean.* Indian claims to supremacy in the ocean that bears its name would be an unmistakable signal of Indian imperialism, especially if it were accompanied by pressure on such island countries as the Seychelles and Maldives. Indian overtures to South Africa and Australia could signify a less aggressive but still ambitious policy of domination in the region. Good Indian relations with Indonesia and other members of the Association of Southeast Asian Nations (ASEAN) would suggest friendly Indian intentions toward Pakistan.

❑ *Indian policy toward the Tamils in Sri Lanka.* After covert assistance to the Tamil rebels in the 1980s, New Delhi has ceased such actions. A renewal of this aid would signify an Indian attempt to gain dominance over Sri Lanka and the rise of Indian imperialism.

❑ *Attitudes toward U.S. military presence on Diego Garcia and American-Pakistani ties.* Indian arguments that the American military and security presence in the Indian Ocean area is a provocation or threat to peace would be a sure sign that India was contemplating some form of expansion or aggression in its region. Indian acceptance of such an American regional role would indicate willingness to live at peace with Pakistan and its other neighbors.

❑ *The size and composition of the navy.* India has greatly reduced its ambitious naval building plans of the 1980s. If India renews its attempts to acquire Indian-built aircraft carriers and nuclear submarines, it would signal Indian attempts to dominate the Indian Ocean. Such developments should be viewed in the context of the Chinese naval presence in the Indian Ocean and the degree of Chinese-Burmese naval cooperation at the time. Indian naval developments should also be assessed in light of Indian relations with South Africa, Indonesia, Australia, and the United States. A lack of Indian naval cooperation with the latter countries and an absence of a Chinese naval threat in the Indian Ocean, combined with a major expansion of the Indian navy, would be a sign of coming Indian aggression.

❑ *The United Nations.* India will undoubtedly seek a permanent Security Council seat if its economy projects it firmly into great-power status. The manner in which India seeks this reorganization of the Security Council will offer indications of India's purposes. India might want to play a constructive role in fostering regional and world peace, or might seek to gain a veto over U.N. attempts to restrain Indian aggression. Depending on international circumstances, Indo-Russian cooperation over such matters would be revealing of the intentions of both countries.

❑ *Activities within the nonaligned movement.* With the collapse of the Soviet Union, the Nonaligned Movement has lost its purpose, except perhaps as a forum for anti-Americanism. If India, a leader in the Movement, attempts to focus it against the United States, it could signify an Indian attempt at hegemony in South Asia and the Indian Ocean.

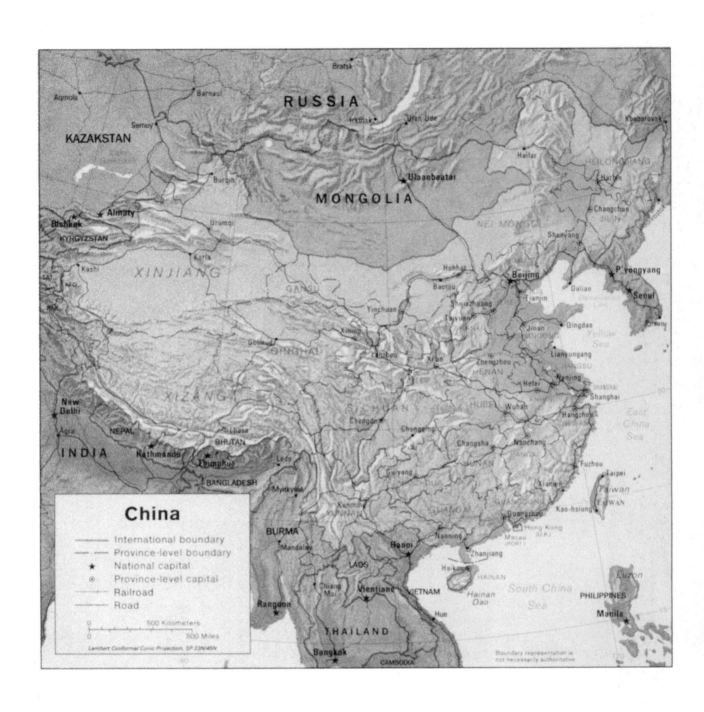

China

- ——— International boundary
- —·—·— Province-level boundary
- ★ National capital
- ⊙ Province-level capital
- ——— Railroad
- ——— Road

0 ____ 500 Kilometers
0 ____ 500 Miles
Lambert Conformal Conic Projection, SP 23N/45N

Boundary representation is
not necessarily authoritative

5. CHINA

The sleeping dragon is awakening and, as Napoleon predicted, the world is beginning to tremble. Given the People's Republic of China's admixture of enormous potential and huge problems, the possibilities for the country in 2015 vary greatly. Whether China emerges as a highly aggressive great power, evolves into a powerful country following a reasonable foreign policy or fails to solve its problems and falls into decline will be one of the two or three most important world events of the next two decades. It is clear, however, that the capitalist reforms of the past 15 years have unleashed revolutionary forces in China. The country is undergoing the greatest political changes since the 1949 Communist victory in the Chinese Civil War.

The obstacles to China becoming a great power are the opposite of India's. If the new Chinese market economy develops too quickly (but unevenly in terms of regional distribution of wealth), the center may lose some control over the provinces because of their growing power relative to that of Beijing. The major reason is that the central government currently lacks the infrastructure, the legal and tax systems, and the financial institutions necessary to collect sufficient revenues from the ever-richer coastal areas and to maintain controls over the national economy. The challenges facing Beijing include raising the living standards of all Chinese in a manner perceived as generally equitable, building an adequate communications and transportation infrastructure, replacing the old social welfare system based on state-owned enterprises with a system compatible with a market economy, arranging a new relationship between the center and the provinces and between rural and the rapidly expanding urban areas, and creating adequate new legal and financial arrangements. Success or failure to achieve these goals will depend greatly on the abilities of the person who will succeed Deng Xiaoping as China's next supreme leader.

Whatever his intentions, the economic reforms initiated by Deng have undermined the dictatorship to a large degree. Deng's successor is almost certain to be an authoritarian rather than a totalitarian leader. Totalitarian governments rely on protecting their monopoly on power by maintaining strict control over the economy. By abandoning such controls and allowing large amounts of private wealth to be accumulated, Deng has permitted independent power centers to be created. Deng still retained considerable personal power, thanks to his reputation as the last of the great revolutionaries. No Communist successor will have such prestige, and therefore will possess less power, or is likely to enjoy Deng's influence with the People's Liberation Army (PLA).

Short of the necessary funds, Deng's government has ordered the PLA to raise part of its own revenues. It is estimated that the PLA now receives less than half its budget from

Beijing, accumulating the rest through commercial ventures. By going into business on a huge scale, the PLA has been seriously degraded as a fighting force. At the same time, its enterprises have wedded some PLA regional commands to the booming provincial economies of the coast. If this process were to continue unchecked, local PLA commanders might not be able or be willing to force the rich provinces back under the strict control of the center. However, the PLA as a whole remains highly nationalistic and would undoubtedly battle to protect China's unity from threats of outright provincial secession. Furthermore, despite the conversion of many units into business enterprises, the PLA still possesses a formidable fighting core. But short of overt national fracture, under some circumstances, the PLA might preserve its own unity by merely observing either a post-Deng succession struggle at the center or a major redistribution of power between Beijing and the provinces.

Chinese Communism is dead as an ideology, and the Party survives only as a tool for national government. The collapse of Soviet Communism and the Chinese reversion to capitalism has thoroughly discredited Marxism in China. The Party has lost its moral authority and is rapidly losing its political authority, as capitalism allows power bases to develop independent of the Party. As a result, Beijing is being deprived of one of its major controls over the provinces.

Lacking the ability to extract sufficient revenues from the richer provinces, Beijing is also losing some control over the poorer inland provinces. It can no longer supply them with the services necessary to command their loyalty. The central government has created a new paramilitary organization, the People's Armed Police (PAP), to maintain order, but Beijing's shortage of funds has made it difficult to sustain this force. Moreover, government bureaucrats and police cannot survive on the low salaries paid by Beijing and are increasingly relying on graft to support themselves. This has tended to discredit the central government, especially in the poor inland provinces, because the inhabitants cannot easily afford to pay bribes for government services or for protection.

Meanwhile, the richer provinces are making trade deals with foreign governments, controlling their own energy supplies, fashioning their own broadcasting systems and building autonomous governments. Most notably, wealthy Guangdong with its 65 million people and an extraordinary annual GNP growth of 20 percent now enjoys considerable autonomy. In several provinces, the tendency toward autonomy has been strengthened further by investments flowing into the coastal provinces from the overseas Chinese communities. The overseas Chinese, largely descended from immigrants from the coastal provinces, in many cases retain strong regional loyalties. They invest not just in China but in the province or even the village of their ancestors. The 50 to 60 million overseas Chinese are estimated to control $1.5 to 2 trillion in assets. A significant portion of this money has flowed back into the coastal provinces over the past 15 years and helps explain the huge boom in the economy of eastern China; such investment increases provincial independence from Beijing's control. Taiwan has played a major role in these developments as a way to try to weaken Beijing's authority and to create a special relationship directly with the southern Chinese coastal provinces. (More quietly, Japan has been doing the same with Japanese money funneled into the northern coastal provinces.) But whether or not these efforts at subversion will succeed remains highly uncertain.

In contrast to the population of the coastal provinces, the 100 million non-Han Chinese national minorities within the PRC now present little danger to the unity of the country. Tibet harbors the strongest nationalist movement, but the 2 million Tibetans are no match for the local PLA garrison. The different ethnic groups in Xinjiang have been more restive since the disintegration of the Soviet union and the independence of the Central Asian Republics; resultant violence has been contained by the PLA and the FAP. However, if the center were to lose enough control over the provinces in some future power struggle, Tibet and Xinjiang might make a bid to break away from the PRC.

Despite the challenges to its control over the country, the central government is exhibiting increasing signs of self confidence. One of the paradoxes confronting China watchers is this contrast between the reality of increasing provincial autonomy and the rhetoric emerging from Beijing. In fact, following Deng's death, a new Chinese leader or leadership may emerge, skillful and forceful enough to wrest back power from the provinces. Even now, the central government is clearly buoyed by its realization of China's astounding surge of economic strength and the prospects that continued growth may propel the country past the United States in terms of GNP sometime in the first quarter of the twenty first century. If the center can channel a part of this national wealth to the PLA, China could roughly balance American military power in 20 to 30 years.

Chinese government spokesmen, diplomats, and military officials increasingly speak of determination to avenge past humiliations of Chinese pride and to use force, if necessary, to defend or assert important territorial claims. In addition to the well-known Chinese claims to the Spratly Islands and to sovereignty over Taiwan, Beijing has certain claims on parts of Kazakhstan, Tajikistan, Kirgizstan and Siberia. Already, the growth in the Chinese economy is exerting a powerful attraction on the ex-Soviet territories along the Chinese border. Illegal Chinese emigration into Siberia and the Russian Far East is also considerable. Previous Russian fears about Japanese designs on Siberia have been replaced by worries about Chinese intentions toward that gigantic, resource-rich but underpopulated region.

As nationalism has replaced communism as the government's ideology, there have been signs of a return by some Chinese officials to old attitudes of superiority. If such attitudes were to become widespread among Chinese leaders at a time when China had become even more powerful, the Chinese could attempt to reduce their small neighbors to protectorate status and to insist on the treatment of China as a superior by India, Russia, and Japan. As a result, China may firmly oppose Indian and Japanese efforts to obtain permanent U.N. Security Council seats. Further, Chinese attempts to ring its abundant borders with a band of friendly states for defensive reasons might be interpreted in New Delhi, Moscow, and Tokyo as creating spheres of influence at Indian, Russian or Japanese expense.

Given the huge and growing Chinese population, the contrasts between the rich east and the poor west, the uncertainties of the post-Deng succession, and the amazing growth of the Chinese economy, the range of possibilities for China in 20 years is enormous.

ALTERNATIVES

1. Weak China

China has enjoyed spectacular economic success over the past 15 years, but the growth of the Chinese economy has been heavily concentrated in the industrial sector; the agricultural sector has grown hardly at all. This imbalance has created tensions between the cities and the countryside that might lead to serious social unrest. If China lacks an *effective central leadership*, it could fail to address these social problems. As a result, industrial growth could falter or cease. Foreign investment, so vital to Chinese development, might slacken or even cease. In that case, China could fall into serious, prolonged economic depression. Popular loyalty to the government could be undermined.

Under such circumstances, the central government still might remain powerful, command the support of the PLA and pursue highly nationalistic policies. Beijing might even seek an international crisis, if only to try to win back the loyalty of the Chinese population. For example, Beijing might create a pretext to confront Taiwan, Vietnam, or Russia, or some neighbor of China's might act provocatively, mistakenly believing that Beijing no longer had the will or means to respond effectively. Whether it provoked a war or was itself provoked, the government might suffer a humiliating defeat. The general population, already restive due to poor economic conditions, might become unruly. Such defiance of the center, followed by the use of the PLA to restore central authority, might set off considerable violence in the Chinese heartland and even trigger revolts in Tibet, Xinjiang and Inner Mongolia.

Such a national crisis might not be resolved quickly or neatly. In 2015, China might be in a state of internal disunity, although not so serious as that of the early 20th century. Organized crime, piracy, and drug trafficking could flourish in some provinces, forcing outside powers to intervene to deal with these threats in coastal regions. The control of Chinese nuclear weapons might be in dispute, creating an even greater danger for the world, but outsiders might be deterred by such weapons from major involvement in Chinese civil turmoil and from attempting to detach pieces of Chinese territory. If agriculture and the distribution of food were disrupted, large parts of the Chinese population might be in danger of starvation. On the other hand, the central government might act decisively, even brutally, in order to restore order.

China's weak economy, the flight of foreign capital, the concentration of the PLA on internal security duties, and lack of support from the general population for the government might leave China unable to pursue an active foreign policy. The PLA would be strong enough to defend China, but China would play no significant role in the affairs of East Asia. Such a China would not be a great power.

2. Provincial China

China might suffer from ineffective or misguided leaders after Deng's death. Nonetheless, parts of China might continue to enjoy significant prosperity. The richer provinces could gain effective autonomy from Beijing before 2015, but national sentiment, fear of foreign powers, desire to avoid civil war and a recognition of the advantages of maintaining some form of central government could result in the formal unity of China being preserved. No formal arrangement for such a system might be developed; instead, Beijing would be involved in a separate, less authoritative, relationship with the richer provinces than with the poorer ones. The richer provinces might pay significant taxes to Beijing but be effectively independent of many forms of central authority. The poorer provinces would be under tighter central control, while struggling to grow wealthy enough to gain more autonomy. The non-Han Chinese areas might remain under firm PLA control, paid for by the richer provinces. Alternatively, Tibet might enjoy no more than a confederal link to Beijing.

Provincial China would have neither a single political system nor a successor to the defunct Communist Party. Some provinces might have authoritarian governments; others might have liberal or political systems. Such a varied political landscape would be inherently unstable, suggesting an evolution to more uniform political arrangements in the future. In 2015, however, whatever the arrangements in the provinces, the central government would remain an authoritarian bureaucracy.

This China might possess a formidable nuclear arsenal, subsidized by all the provinces as a form of protection, but Beijing's ability to project conventional force beyond its borders might be quite limited. The richer provinces might have their own militia forces to deal with piracy, smuggling and border control. In a vague way, Provincial China might resemble the Japan of the 1980s: a great power only economically. However, lack of an effective nation-wide system of laws, banks, courts, transport, welfare, and other components of modern capitalism could inhibit the continuation of high rates of economic growth, and China would not realize its full potential.

Such a China would probably enjoy amicable relations with its neighbors, based on the coastal provinces' desire for protecting their trade and prosperity. Such circumstances would make it easy for Taiwan to negotiate a formal submission to rule from Beijing, while enjoying almost the same degree of independence it presently has. Provincial China might even welcome a strong American presence in East Asia and the Pacific as a form of protection against both Japan and Russia. The degree of Chinese prosperity, the willingness of the richer provinces to contribute to national defense and the relative power of the Russian armed forces would determine the nature of the Russian-Chinese relationship. So would the degree to which Chinese security and prosperity mattered to Japan and the United States, who might even serve as Provincial China's active protectors against a predatory Russia. On the other hand, a severe enough threat from Russia might be the impetus to lead the Chinese to transform their country into a true federal state or even to accept a new form of authoritarian central rule.

3. Liberal China

By 2015, China could be in the process of moving toward the establishment of a multiparty elected system of government, something like that of Western European states in the mid-19th century. Beijing's leaders would be concerned about achieving popular support, recognizing the enhanced power gained from having a willing national consensus to carry out policies. A Liberal Chinese political system would undoubtedly be imposed from above, unlike the process in the United States in 1787-88. China would remain quasi-authoritarian in some ways but the foundation would have been laid for evolution into a broadly liberal and, eventually, into a democratic state. In 2015, however, China would hardly be democratic, although power would be shared between the central and provincial governments, basic human and civil rights would be protected, and all Chinese would live under the firm rule of law.

The central government of such a China would remain highly concerned with strong defense, active foreign policy, and some regulation of the national economy. Such a wealthy, internally peaceful, culturally, and intellectually dynamic China would produce self-confident but not unreasonable leaders. They would prove willing to compromise with other great powers over conflicts and carry out a cooperative foreign policy to maintain world peace. But China would strongly assert itself when it felt its rights threatened—and it would have a rather nationalistic sense of what its rights were. After the liberal political system had been erected, Beijing could resolve the issues of revenue collection and distribution, pass laws to govern the economy and create the other prerequisites for a well-functioning capitalist system. This would allow for continued high rates of growth, social peace, and heavy government spending.

Chinese culture lacks a Western legal tradition, the necessary precondition for an effective federal system. However, given unprecedented Chinese access to ideas from the outside world and the sweeping changes possible in a prosperous post-Communist China, the Chinese might still conduct a successful political-legal-administrative transformation of their governmental structures. A federal system would provide an ideal means to regulate relations between the provinces and the center, and among the provinces. However, even if the Chinese were to adopt such a system, it would be a Chinese adaptation of federalism to their conditions, not an imitation of Western systems. Such a China would be strong enough to use force if Taiwan were to seek full independence. It would repress independence movements in Tibet and Xinjiang, although it might give those regions a form of limited autonomy within a federal system. It might seek predominance in East Asia by a combination of economic and military strength, but without crudely bullying its neighbors. Russian, Japanese, Indian, and American influence in Central and Southeast Asia and Korea might be resisted and resented, but Beijing would try to avoid disrupting the trade upon which its prosperity would rest.

4. Authoritarian China

Nationalism may replace Communism as a burning political faith for the Chinese. A post-Deng government might produce one or more charismatic, authoritarian leaders who could mobilize the loyalty of the Chinese people, direct continued vigorous economic growth and resolve distribution of power questions very much in favor of Beijing. Such a China could be very dangerous. It might be motivated by the type of aggressive need to assert itself that afflicted Italy, Germany and Japan before World War II. Or it might simply view attempts to bring China into a cooperative relationship with the other great powers as an infringement on its sovereignty. Beijing might be involved in a continuous series of confrontations, one of which might spark an armed conflict. Such a China could take advantage of a vigorous economy to pour large amounts of money into the armed forces and then embark on an offensive foreign policy, seeking undisputed predominance in Asia. By 2015, such a China could be seeking to become a truly global power.

If an authoritarian China were confronted by an imperial Russia, a major war between the two could follow. If India were allied to Russia at the time, all mainland Asia might be dragged into the conflict. On the other hand, if Russia presented no threat to China, strong nationalism still might motivate Beijing to attempt to recover the territories north of Manchuria lost to Russia in the so-called "Unequal Treaties" of the nineteenth century. A militarist, expansionist China could drive Russia, Japan, Indonesia, and India into an anti-Chinese alliance designed to contain Beijing's expansionism. Such a coalition could be supported and even joined by the United States.

If an authoritarian China could create the legal, administrative, social and financial structures necessary to sustain economic growth in a modern market economy, the Chinese government might enjoy the world's largest national budget by 2015. Under some circumstances, China might present a significant menace to world peace. True, an authoritarian China would not be driven by ideology to try to conquer the world as the

Nazis or Communists were. But Chinese nationalists could be motivated by old resentments to settle scores with the Russians, Vietnamese, Indonesians, Indians, and Americans. If China proved victorious, it would be hegemon over Eurasia. Even if China demanded no more than recognition of its supremacy in the Eastern Hemisphere, this could present a threat to the security and prosperity of Japan or the United States.

INDICATORS

The list of indicators that follow provide ways to make educated guesses about the direction in which China may be headed.

- ❑ *A popular democratic movement.* Such a political phenomenon would lead to revolutionary changes in every aspect of Chinese society. In the short run, a transformation to democracy would probably convulse China through internal conflict. If the forces of democracy won, China would emerge as an extremely dynamic state. Filled with a youthful enthusiasm, it would likely rise to preeminence among the great powers.

- ❑ *Emergence of a charismatic national leader.* Given the threats that exist to Chinese unity and to the creation of a national consensus, an inspiring leader could concentrate the country's resources and energies in dramatic ways. Such a leader might be a force for good or evil. But he would likely make China a more significant international force than it would be otherwise.

- ❑ *Air, water, and soil quality.* In many ways, the development of the Chinese economy resembles the environmentally destructive process carried out in nineteenth-century Europe. But given its limited arable land and the heavy concentration of the Chinese population, such methods will produce catastrophe if not checked. China will have a population of about 1.5 billion people by 2015. The more the Chinese degrade their soil and water, the more food they will be forced to import. True, the Chinese may pay for food imports by industrial production, but if the process creates unbreathable air in overcrowded cities, the Chinese will be caught in a vicious circle. If the Chinese do not drastically reduce the damage they are inflicting on their environment, they will suffer social and economic disaster.

- ❑ *Chinese oil supplies.* Continued Chinese economic development will require ever larger amounts of oil. The Chinese may discover enough new petroleum sources in the Tarim Basin, other inland fields, or in undisputed offshore areas. Under such circumstances, its economic prospects would improve greatly without disrupting China's relations with neighboring states. But discovery of oil in disputed areas off the Chinese coast, especially in the South China Sea, might involve China in conflict with its neighbors, sharply heighten tensions in East Asia, and prompt a major regional arms race. If China remains dependent on imports of Middle East oil, particularly if its needs increase dramatically, the Chinese will undoubtedly begin a major expansion of their navy. Given Chinese vulnerability under such circumstances to having its SLOCs cut, India and Indonesia would probably also expand their navies significantly. In other words, the prospects for peace in Asia over the next 20 years could be enhanced if the Chinese discover oil in areas under their uncontested control, but much would depend on the type of China that exists in the 2015 period. If China becomes highly nationalistic, secure oil supplies would enhance its power yet also endanger Asian security from the period 2010 onward.

❑ *Creation of a federal system.* A formal division of powers between the central government and the provinces, and the creation of an effective revenue collecting system would indicate a growing degree of control by Beijing over the country. It would also provide the basis for a greater flow of funds to the armed forces.

❑ *Willingness to join and participate in international organizations.* The Chinese government has shown little interest in joining such organizations, apparently seeing them as offering restraints on Chinese sovereignty. Nor has it shown much enthusiasm for United Nations peace operations. A positive change in Chinese attitudes toward the United Nations, the ASEAN Regional Forum, or a new subregional security organ would signal that China was making major efforts to ensure regional and world peace.

❑ *Closer economic interdependence between China and Taiwan.* The more that the prosperity of the two countries becomes intertwined, the less the danger of an armed conflict between the two.

❑ *Declaration of independence by Taiwan.* Under almost any circumstances, this would trigger an armed response from China. If China were unable to respond with force, it would indicate a severe weakening of central authority.

❑ *Separatism in Central Asia.* Greater restiveness in Xinjiang, Tibet and Inner Mongolia would indicate a breakdown in central authority or the inability of the central government to provide services or subsidies to the outlying regions.

❑ *Resolution of the Korean problem.* The degree to which China helps or hinders the peaceful resolution of the North Korean nuclear issue and aids or obstructs Korean unification will be highly indicative of Chinese benevolence or hostility toward the United States and Japan. If China seeks to dominate a united Korea, it would suggest an attempt to use that country against Japan.

❑ *Increased activity by secret societies, piracy and drug trafficking.* Crime is on the rise in China. One indication of a change in the balance of power between the central government and the provinces is the amount of major crime that can flourish in the absence of effective central police powers. High rates of major crime, particularly kinds that effect commerce and transport, would also indicate brakes on the Chinese economy. More public activity by organized criminal entities such as the "Triads" would indicate other signs of the reduction of Beijing's power.

❑ *Violation of trade agreements between the central government and foreign states.* Many of the recent Chinese trade violations are not the fault of the Beijing regime. Rather, they indicate decisions on the provincial level or the influence of Hong Kong, Taiwan, and Japan on the provincial economies. But an increase in such violations would indicate that the authority of the central government was being further eroded.

❑ *The Transformation of ASEAN into a collective defense organization.* ASEAN has shown little ability to transform itself into the NATO of Southeast Asia because of the nationalism of its individual members. If the organization put aside suchconsiderations in the cause of common defense, however, it could suggest a severe Chinese threat to the region.

❑ *The sale or transfer of nuclear weapons and/or ballistic missile technology.* Continued Chinese activities along these lines can be interpreted as extremely hostile to the United States. The Chinese have made it plain that the more countries that possess weapons of mass destruction, the more it inhibits the United States from using its power.

❑ *A naval buildup.* If the Chinese begin a major naval armaments program, especially to produce aircraft carriers, nuclear submarines, and cruisers, it would suggest at least an attempt to put pressure on Japan, the Southeast Asian states, and India.

❑ *The development of an amphibious warfare capability.* At present, the Chinese armed forces possess little ability to invade Taiwan or to project military power into the Southeast Asian islands. If the armed forces embark on programs to improve such capabilities, particularly by creating a large amphibious force, it could indicate aggressive intentions on the part of the Chinese government.

❑ *Chinese arms sales in Southeast Asia.* The quality of Chinese conventional arms has been low. If there is a significant increase in the volume of Chinese conventional arms sales in Southeast Asia, it would indicate either a considerable increase in Chinese influence in the region or a great improvement in the quality of Chinese military equipment.

❑ *Relations between Israel and China.* Israel has been willing to give China considerable access to Israeli advanced military technology. As a *quid pro quo, the* Chinese have limited the sale of arms to Israel's enemies. But China may grow increasingly dependent on imports of Middle East oil and seek ways to improve its relations with the Arab states. The nature of Israeli-Chinese relations would provide evidence of the state of both Chinese energy supplies and of its attempts to upgrade the quality of its armaments.

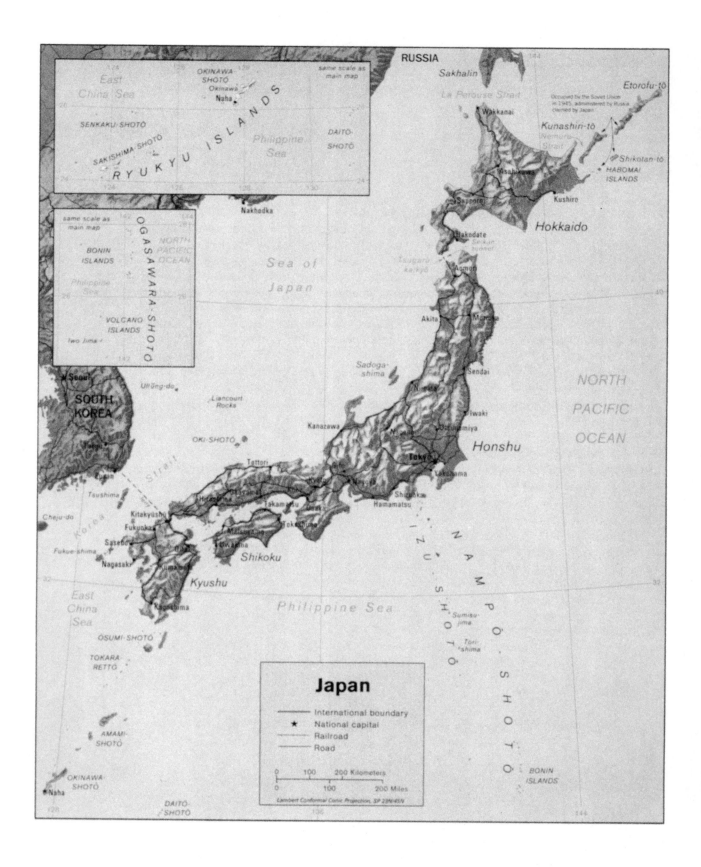

RUSSIA

East
China Sea

OKINAWA-
SHOTŌ
Okinawa

Naha

same scale as
main map

Sakhalin

La Pérouse Strait

Etorofu-tō

Occupied by the Soviet Union
in 1945, administered by Russia,
claimed by Japan.

Wakkanai

Kunashiri-tō

Nemuro
Strait

Shikotan-tō

HABOMAI
ISLANDS

SENKAKU-SHOTŌ

SAKISHIMA-SHOTŌ

Philippine
Sea

DAITŌ-
SHOTŌ

Asahikawa

Kushiro

R Y U K Y U   I S L A N D S

Sapporo

Hokkaido

Nakhodka

same scale as
main map

OGASAWARA-SHOTŌ

NORTH
PACIFIC
OCEAN

Hakodate

Seikan
tunnel

BONIN
ISLANDS

Philippine
Sea

Sea of
Japan

Tsugaru
kaikyō

Aomori

VOLCANO
ISLANDS

Akita

Morioka

Iwo Jima

Sadoga-
shima

Sendai

Niigata

★ Seoul

Ullŭng-do

SOUTH
KOREA

Liancourt
Rocks

Iwaki

Utsunomiya

NORTH

Kanazawa

Nagano

PACIFIC

Taegu

OKI-SHOTŌ

Tōkyō

Yokohama

Honshu

OCEAN

Pusan

Korea Strait

Tottori

Shizuoka

Tsushima

Hiroshima

Okayama

Takamatsu

Hamamatsu

Cheju-do

Kitakyūshū

Matsuyama

Tokushima

Fukuoka

Shikoku

N A M P O - S H O T Ō

Fukue-shima

Sasebo

Ōita

Nagasaki

Ōita

Kyushu

Kagoshima

Sumisu-
jima

East
China
Sea

Philippine Sea

Tori-
shima

ŌSUMI-SHOTŌ

TOKARA-
RETTŌ

N A M P O - S H O T Ō

AMAMI-
SHOTŌ

Japan

International boundary

★   National capital

Railroad

Road

BONIN
ISLANDS

OKINAWA-
SHOTŌ

Naha

0   100   200 Kilometers

0   100   200 Miles

DAITŌ-
SHOTŌ

Lambert Conformal Conic Projection, SP 23N/45N

6. JAPAN

Rich, politically stable, technologically advanced, protected by surrounding seas and a large modern navy, allied to the United States, the world's paramount power, Japan would appear to be certain to enjoy security and strength in 2015. Nonetheless, the Japanese have many worries about their future. The end of the Cold War, signs of isolationism in the United States and American-Japanese friction over trade imbalances raise questions about the duration of the American-Japanese security relationship. These concerns are heightened by the strong possibility that China will be a major economic and military power in fewer than 20 years. China could possibly be overwhelmed by its huge and growing population, but Japan faces the opposite problem. In 2015, its inhabitants will number only about 135 million, less than one-tenth of the Chinese population at the time. Furthermore, the Japanese population will be aging, the Chinese population youthful. China could conceivably outnumber Japan in military-age manpower by a ratio of fifteen to one.

Given its high density of population in a few urban areas, Japan is extremely vulnerable to nuclear attack. As few as three or four thermonuclear explosions could totally devastate Japan. To inflict equivalent damage on Russia or China, Japan would need to hit back with 100 or more warheads. Japan is almost as vulnerable against conventional attack, lacking strategic depth and possessing a long, vulnerable coastline. As World War II demonstrated, at a time when Japan was far less dependent on imports than it will be over the next 20 years, it is also vulnerable to blockade and to interruption of its SLOCs. The Japanese would be hard pressed to build a navy large enough to protect them and such an effort would cause major economic dislocations. Thus, even the faint possibility of an end to the American defense of Japan is enough to cause worry.

Japanese competitiveness is decreasing for myriad reasons, including a graying population, rising welfare, social security and health costs. But the principal challenge to Japanese competitiveness may stem from Japan's unprecedented overinvestment in its financial and corporate markets and the yen's overappreciation. These facts force an excessive allocation of resources towards production and away from domestic consumption, despite the younger generation's demand for more comforts and less toil than their hardworking parents and grandparents experienced. Much increased travel abroad over the past 10 years has made it clear to the Japanese that their lives are far harder than in supposedly poorer European and North American countries. Thus, the end to monolithic Liberal Democratic party rule and the emergence of a true multiparty system are also a threat to Japanese competitiveness.

Although both defense spending and military activity continue to face severe political restraints in Japan, the emergence of a multiparty system may eventually lead to an marked increase in the size, mission and capability of the Japanese Self Defense Forces. The Socialists, the party representing the core of Japanese antimilitary and pro-isolationist sentiments, have already largely abandoned these attitudes in order to remain a political force. More significant is that, despite deep-seated pacifism among most Japanese adults, younger Japanese do not have personal memories of the Second World War or the hard years of the Occupation. They are far more willing for Japan to act as a "normal country," with "multidimensional" powers, within certain cautious limits. The older Japanese bureaucracy is even more cautious in such matters. Nonetheless, it seems very likely that the Japanese constitution will be reinterpreted, and possibly amended, in the next 10 to 15 years, in order to permit the government more freedom in defense matters and in the use of armed force.

But there seems to be no question that, regardless of Japanese foreign and security policy over the next 20 years, Japan will remain a healthy democracy. In fact, as the outline of a stable multiparty system emerges after two or more general elections, Japan is likely to embark on the next century as one of the world's great free-market democracies.

The continuing possibility of upheaval on the Korean peninsula, as well as the longer-term possibility of a united and nuclear-armed Korea, is also pushing the Japanese toward a strengthening of their armed forces, greater participation in regional and world affairs, and a desire to gain a permanent seat on the Security Council. Korean-Japanese antagonism remains strong, and many Japanese think that they can no longer be certain of indefinite American protection and mediation between them and the Koreans. The more Japan enjoys the attributes of a normal great power, the less reason it has to fear Korea or even a possible anti-Japanese Korean-Chinese alliance. However, the possibility of such a coalition aimed at Japan undoubtedly has made some Japanese think seriously about the security implications.

Another motive for major Japanese increases in defense spending is their worry over the future of Russia. Either the breakup of Russia or its return to imperialism would threaten Japanese interests. Russia remains the world's major potential source of nuclear proliferation. In the longer term, the disintegration of Russia would remove a significant counterweight to Chinese military power in Asia. On the other hand, given the historic hostility between Russians and Japanese and the ongoing Japanese claims to the Russian-occupied southern Kuriles, an expansionist Russia would be perceived as a grave threat in Japan.

The Sino-Japanese relationship could very well replace that between Japan and the United States as the most important concern of Japanese foreign policy by 2015. This could be true, even if the American-Japanese security relationship were strengthened in response to a Chinese military threat. The growth of the Chinese economy is paralleled by the growth of Sino-Japanese economic links; a stable and prosperous China is in the Japanese national interest. But if the Chinese economy does advance to the degree that some analysts predict by 2015, it would dwarf and even threaten the Japanese economy. A rich China would almost certainly be a very powerful China. Underneath even the closest economic cooperation between such a China and Japan, mutual antagonism and competition would remain strong. Japan will have to learn how to manage such arelationship on its own. For the moment, at least, Chinese leaders are very skillful at manipulating the historic legacy of Japanese guilt to their own ends.

The trauma of 1945 continues to make the Japanese extremely uncertain of the degree to which they can trust themselves to behave rationally in an independent national manner. The Japanese are probably even more aware than foreigners of how strong Japanese nationalism, racism, and xenophobia still are. But as uncomfortable as the Japanese are at making their own decisions and acting as world leaders, they will have little choice over the next two decades. Despite great efforts to avoid it, the Japanese must now import rice, a fact with immense symbolic meaning for the Japanese. Seafood is becoming more scarce in nearby Japanese waters and must be harvested in sea areas claimed by others. As mentioned, although the degree of interdependence between the Japanese and Chinese economies is growing greater by the day, Japan cannot afford to lose its American markets. Thus, even to feed themselves and their industries, the Japanese will depend on good relations with China, Korea, Russia, Taiwan, and the United States.

The Japanese face tremendous pressure not to remain neutral in case of a conflict on the Korean peninsula or a crisis between China and Taiwan or between China and the United States. Nor can they necessarily just follow the American lead in such circumstances. Japanese and American interests might differ too greatly. There are a number of signs that the Japanese leadership is quite aware of the need to forge a completely independent foreign and security policy. Already, in the past 5 years or so, East Asians have been noting a far greater degree of Japanese assertiveness than at any time since 1945. This change in attitude is beginning to penetrate into the average Japanese mentality, although it may take a decade or longer to make a significant difference.

Nonetheless, even if Japan assumes all the responsibilities of a completely sovereign state and takes on all the characteristics of a great power, it likely will seek to maintain its close security relationship with the United States. The Japanese will remain aware that any alternative to the preservation of the American-Japanese alliance offers them far more disadvantages than advantages. What is far less certain is whether or not the United States will preserve that relationship. Thus, there are several alternative possibilities for the future of Japan in 2015.

ALTERNATIVES

1. Japan, an American Ally

Japan might remain allied to the United States, but the partnership would probably be a far more equal one—although still probably not more symmetrical in 2015. In cooperation with its ally, Japan might have acquired a theater antimissile defense system and could maintain a reconnaissance satellite system. The American naval presence in the Western Pacific could have relatively diminished capability next to that of the Japanese Maritime Self-Defense Force. Japan may not have any other formal military alliances, but it probably would have close ties to the ASEAN states and would cooperate militarily with several of them, especially Thailand and Indonesia. Japanese-Australian security cooperation could also be close. And, depending on the challenge posed by either Russia or China, Japan could even have a cooperative military relationship with Seoul.

The Japanese constitution could have been reinterpreted to allow combat operations in the event of regional crises, but the prohibition of war as an instrument of national policy would probably be maintained (a more symbolic gesture than one of real value.). Japan would have gained a permanent seat on the Security Council and would participate routinely in U.N. military operations, but to offset its increased power projection capabilities, the Japanese government would try to avoid any military measures that upset its neighbors. In particular, the Japanese would be very solicitous of Chinese feelings. Because of the increase in the size of the Japanese navy over the previous 20 years, Japan would try to avoid actions suggesting cooperation with the Indian or Indonesian navies to threaten Chinese SLOCs.

Japan would respond to a Chinese or Korean threat by adhering more closely with the United States, but the Japanese would do nothing militarily to take advantage of Chinese or Korean weaknesses, in case problems developed on the Asian mainland. Unless China proved vulnerable, Japan would avoid involvement in any Russo-Chinese imbroglio. If the United States did become involved, Japan would offer diplomatic and economic support, but would avoid committing forces of its own. Only in the case of dire threat from China would Japan take decisive action on its own. This might involve taking part in an anti-Chinese alliance linking Japan to Indonesia, India, Russia, possibly Korea, and possibly the United States as a full member of the coalition. The United States would usually defer to Japanese interests in Asia, and Japan would follow the American lead in other parts of the world.

Despite its alliance with the United States, this Japan might have closer economic ties with China. The Chinese economy might have grown larger than the American and the volume of Sino-Japanese trade might exceed that between the United States and Japan. Furthermore, Japan might be extending China a great deal of technical assistance to control pollution, to increase crop yields, to improve transport and communications and to conduct geological surveys. The Japanese also might do what they could to encourage liberalization and democratization in China. The more China approached the status of a liberal democratic consumer society, the better it would be for Japanese security and prosperity.

To an extent, Japan would be enhancing its independence by balancing its security relationship to the United States with its economic and political relationship with China. China, as the rising power, would undoubtedly find it beneficial to play the world's two leading free-market democracies against one another. Whenever serious American-Chinese friction threatened, Japan might offer itself as the mediator. To a great extent, the peace of the world would rest on the triangular Beijing-Tokyo-Washington balance of economic and military power.

2. A Renationalized Japan

For a variety of reasons, the U.S.-Japan security relationship might not survive until 2015. Under such circumstances, Japan would have to see to its own defense. So long as the American-Japanese relationship was not a hostile one and Japan did not feel particularly threatened by Russia or China, Japanese rearmament might be held within moderate limits, at least at first. But the very fact that Japan had decoupled from the United States might create great fear in East Asia and prompt a regional arms buildup. In turn, particularly if Korean and Chinese armament levels upset Japanese public opinion, a full-scale arms race might break out in East Asia. Japan and China might seek allies against each other and all Asia might be divided into two mutually hostile coalitions.

Historical and cultural attitudes could determine how East Asia would divide. Those countries that had suffered most at Japanese hands before or during World War II or had close cultural ties with China would likely side with Beijing: Korea, Singapore, the Philippines, Cambodia, and Burma. Countries with close economic ties to Japan, with populations of strong anti-Chinese bias, or with reason to fear Beijing might side with Japan: Indonesia, Vietnam, Laos and Thailand. Some countries like Taiwan or Malaysia would try desperately to remain neutral but might find that impossible.

Under the circumstances, it would be likely that Japan would acquire weapons of mass destruction. While the Japanese might consider alliance with a nuclear power like Russia or India as an alternative, their experience with the United States as an ally would almost certainly dissuade them. As a way to try to minimize the impact of such a move on the Japanese population and to reduce the chances of a Chinese nuclear strike against Japanese territory, the Japanese might base their weapons of mass destruction entirely in space.

Japan might try to surround China with a coalition of Indonesia, India, Russia and itself. Given its manpower shortages but technological and economic advantages, the major Japanese contributions to the alliance would be money and its air, maritime and space forces. The Russians and Indians would provide the bulk of the land forces. The Japanese navy, along with those of Indonesia and India, would threaten China with the interruption of its access to outside oil supplies. Japan would likely build nuclear submarines and aircraft carriers.

Given the preexisting antagonisms between China and Japan, such a bipolar division of Asia would be very dangerous, particularly if the United States reduced its military engagement in the region. If one or the other country sensed an imminent change in the balance of power between them, fear could trigger a conflict. The results might prove disastrous for the entire world.

3. Japan, A Great Power

Japan might retain its alliance with the United States but still pursue far more autonomous foreign and security policies than it has over the past 50 years. Suspicions about anti-Japanese feelings in the United States, anti-American feelings in Japan, trade friction, fear that the United States might come to see China as a more valuable partner than Japan, increased Japanese national pride, and a sense that American society was slowly decaying might all combine to lessen Japanese respect for the United States and raise doubts about its reliability. But the Japanese are prudent—they might consider the continuation of the American-Japanese security relationship useful for the moment and dangerous to end abruptly. At the same time, the Japanese might take steps to allow them to break with the United States and provide for their own defense, if necessary.

The resulting American-Japanese relationship might be marked by a peculiar mixture of honesty and deceit, of cooperation and rivalry. The Japanese might greatly expand their intelligence organizations and create an independent surveillance satellite system, relying far less on American support in these matters. They might conduct major offensive intelligence operations in the United States. The Japanese might engage in covert cooperation with the Russians and Chinese, sometimes to the detriment of American interests. The Japanese might hide the true size of their defense spending from the Americans, burying military expenses in the budgets of other agencies and ministries. At the same time, to alleviate

American concerns about burden sharing, the Japanese could still greatly increase their participation in their own defense, particularly by an expansion of their fleet. The reach of the Japanese navy could be extended far beyond the 1,000-mile limit. The navy might purchase sea-control carriers and sealift ships and the air force might acquire long-range transport and aerial refueling capabilities The Japanese might even begin a covert nuclear weapons program, or perhaps a new kind of unconventional weapon of mass destruction, as insurance against a collapse of their alliance with the Americans.

Yet the Japanese might continue to rely heavily on the American nuclear umbrella and on the U.S. Navy for protection. Japan could benefit in its relations with other Asian countries from the appearance of being kept under control by the Americans. Japanese defense expenditures might rise above the virtually sacred limit of one percent of GNP, but still not to the level of American expenditures, thereby saving the Japanese a great deal of money. In case of serious threats to American and Japanese interests in the Western Pacific, the two countries could still rally to each other's assistance, but in the ordinary course of events, the allies might be quite competitive. Such a relationship might continue indefinitely past 2015. Or it might mark a station on the Japanese road to renationalization. Much would depend on the degree to which China might challenge Japan and Japanese perceptions of American reliability in such a case.

INDICATORS

Some indicators can be listed to help gauge the future toward which Japan is going.

❑ *A stable two-party political system.* As the next few elections test and promote recent electoral reforms, the outline of a stable multi-party democratic system may take hold in Japan as it begins the twenty-first century. If so, this development could make it easier for Japan to gradually expand its contributions to regional and global security.

❑ *The acquisition of "balanced" self-defense force capabilities.* If the SDF shifts its priorities to the acquisition of more "balanced" capabilities, permitting more autonomous military capabilities, this could presage a more assertive Japan in regional or global affairs. Such capabilities—e.g., long-range airlift, sealift, theater missile defense, etc.—could be advantageous to U.S. interests if they were developed and used within the context of the U.S.-Japan Mutual Security Treaty and did not unduly upset Japan's neighbors.

❑ *Increasing frictions in the Japan-United States security relationship.* Despite growing tensions over the trade imbalance and other economic issues, the U.S.-Japan security relationship has remained healthy. Nonetheless, there increasingly could be spillover from economic tensions into the security relationship. Even if a $60 billion trade imbalance is not deemed to be significant in economic terms, it would be bound to have a corrosive effect on the long-term viability of the alliance. Similarly, growing tensions over security or political issues--such as the production of Japan's FSX fighter, two-way technology flow, regional security architecture, or alliance roles and missions--could also indicate that the alliance was facing serious trouble.

❑ *Japanese breakthroughs in technology.* If the Japanese were to succeed in solving one or more of their major national problems with a dramatic advance in technology, their power and independence could significantly increase. Some examples of developments that would greatly alter Japan's international status include cold fusion power, superconductivity and robotics. These particular advances in technology would end Japanese dependence on imported oil and solve problems caused by Japan's manpower shortages. Japanese economic and military power would be greatly enhanced and it might detach itself from its close relationship with the United States as a result.

❑ *Japanese behavior during a major crisis*. The degree to which Japan supported or opposed American policies during such threats to the peace of East Asia as a major crisis on the Korean Peninsula or between Taiwan and China would provide major evidence of Japanese attitudes toward the United States, China and their own security. If the American and Japanese responses to a major regional or international crisis was at sharp variance, then the result would likely be to promote major political change in Japan and to accelerate Japan as a more normal nation. Depending on the dexterity of leaders managing the alliance, such political change could be either a fillip to the bilateral alliance or lead to its abrupt demise.

❑ *A Japanese nuclear weapons program*. The significance of such a drastic change in Japanese policy would be self-evident. Presumably such a departure from Japan's postwar policy of three non-nuclear principles would be preceded by the perceived failure or termination of the U.S. nuclear umbrella to Japan. It is hard to imagine how an independent nuclear option on the part of Japan could be anything but highly destabilizing.

❑ *A covert military space program*. A clandestine military space program would indicate that the Japanese no longer believed that they could rely on the United States for protection or the sharing of satellite intelligence. The development of "dual-use" space technology by the Japanese would indicate an attempt to hide their plans for military uses of space.

❑ *Embellished portrayal of national symbols*. The degree to which the Japanese Emperor acts and is treated as a typical constitutional head of state is significant. Any increase of Emperor worship or even excessively reverential treatment would be a sign of growing Japanese nationalism. The more the truth is admitted about Hirohito's role in approving Japanese aggression in the 1930s and 1940s, the better it would be from the American perspective. But a distinction between justifications for Japanese aggression against the Chinese and the West would be of particular significance. Moreover, increasing visits by Japanese officials to the Yasukuni Shrine, especially by defense and foreign ministry officials, would indicate disregard for Chinese, Korean and American sensitivities and possibly indicate a dangerous rise in Japanese militarism.

❑ *The sale of Japanese weapons abroad*. A departure from Japan's postwar policy prohibiting the sale of weapons abroad (other than to the United States) would suggest a far more confident and nationalistic Japan. Such a policy could concomitantly be the result of U.S. pressure to see Japan play a more active security role and also signify that the Japanese were preparing to erect a security system independent of the United States. The more arms—or even information-based technologies that could support modern military forces—the Japanese sold abroad, the

more of a danger signal it would represent. Sales to enemies of the
United States in the Middle East would be particularly significant.

- ❑ *A greatly increased intelligence capability.* This may or may not be another sign
  that the Japanese were preparing to separate from the United States. Once again, the
  key would be whether or not the Japanese shared their intelligence with us. Similarly,
  the enhancement of indigenous weapons programs would suggest that the Japanese
  were losing trust in the United States and were preparing to be fully independent of
  American arms sources.

- ❑ *Rescindment of the tacit 1-percent-of-GNP limit on defense spending.* This could
  represent a major sign of an increase in Japanese nationalism and self-confidence.
  Depending on the circumstances, if the increases were great enough, it would indicate
  a resurgence of Japanese militarism and aggression. But clearly this would depend on
  the level of threat--for instance, from an assertive China—and the degree to which it
  was done within the context of the bilateral security framework.

- ❑ *The creation of a true general staff and/or the upgrading of the defense agency to
  ministry level.* Such moves could be made only with the approval of the Japanese
  people. They would indicate a great upsurge in national feeling, a great sense of
  vulnerability, or both. Since the United States has opposed the elevation of the Defense
  Agency, such a decision could be interpreted as anti-American.

- ❑ *The degree of Japanese investment in China.* The signals that such high investment
  would offer would depend on Chinese foreign and security policies. If these investments
  went to an aggressive China, they might indicate Japan was forging a relationship
  with China at American expense. In times of good Chinese behavior, such investments
  would indicate a Japanese attempt to create a healthy, restraining influence on China.

- ❑ *Elevation to permanent United Nations Security Council membership.* Such an
  event would signal that Japan had become a normal nation again. Recently, Japanese
  diplomats have come close to demanding a seat but insisting that they are remorseful
  for Japan's aggression against China and for its responsibility for starting the Great
  Pacific War. A real indicator of where Japan is headed would be their actions and
  attitudes once ensconced permanently in the Security Council. Obviously, if the
  Japanese acquire their seat, they would be obliged to participate in U.N. military
  operations. But Japanese behavior during such missions would be highly suggestive.
  One tendency to watch for would be Japanese use of such missions to camouflage
  nationalistic intervention in Asian affairs. How would the Japanese use their veto? If
  they opposed the United States in the Security Council, the frequency of the use of the
  Japanese veto and issues over which they employed it would be very illustrative of their
  foreign and security policy intentions.

- ❑ *The return of the southern Kurile Islands to Japan.* For Russia to do this would
  indicate that Russia was in great need of Japanese assistance and that the Japanese
  had indicated that they were prepared to grant such aid. Such an event might signal a
  decision by Russia and Japan to cooperate against China.

- ❑ *Increased Japanese naval cooperation with Indonesia and India.* This would also
  indicate Japanese preparations for cooperation against China. But if such joint

training exercises or other cooperation took place while India was demanding American withdrawal from Diego Garcia, it would suggest strongly a Japanese return to the doctrine of "Asia for the Asians," a thinly disguised version of Japanese neo-imperialism.

NOTES

1.   See Francis Fukuyama, *The End of History and the Last Man* (New York: The Free Press, 1992), 338-9. Fukuyama argues that " a universal and directional history leading up to liberal democracy" may be approaching.

2.   Samuel P. Huntington, "The Clash of Civilizations?", *Foreign Affairs* (Summer 1993), p 48. Huntington writes that "violent conflicts between groups in different civilizations are the most likely and most dangerous source of escalation that could lead to global wars; the paramount axis of world politics will be the relations between 'the West and the Rest'; ... [and] a central focus of conflict for the immediate future will be between the West and several Islamic-Confucian states."

3.   Bruce Russett, *Grasping the Democratic Peace: Principles for a Post-Cold War World* (Princeton, New Jersey: Princeton University Press, 1993) p. 119. Russett states that "Compared with their actions toward other kinds of states, democracies in the modern world are unlikely to engage in militarized disputes with each other. When they do get into disputes with each other, they are less likely to let the disputes escalate. They rarely fight each other even at low levels of lethal violence, and never (or almost never) go to war against each other."

4.   Robert D. Kaplan, "The Coming Anarchy," *The Atlantic Monthly* (February 1994). Kaplan's thesis is that "the coming anarchy" of the developing world will be "*the* national-security issue of the early 21st century."

5.   The fifteen of 1995, plus Poland, the Czech Republic, Slovakia, Hungary, Slovenia, the Baltic Republics and Norway, seem the most likely candidates. Others include Switzerland, Malta, Cyprus, Romania and Bulgaria.

6.   These could include some of the states mentioned at the end of the preceding footnote, plus Croatia, Albania, Serbia, Belarus, Ukraine, and Bosnia, Macedonia and Moldova, if the latter still existed. The possibility of Russia, Turkey and Georgia joining a European Confederation should not be excluded absolutely.

II. ENVIRONMENT

Patrick L. Clawson is a Senior Fellow at the Institute for National Strategic Studies and the author of *Iran's Strategic Intentions and Capabilities* (McNair Paper 29); *Iran's Challenge to the West* (1993); and *Uprooting Leninism, Cultivating Liberty*, with Vladimir Tsmaneanu (1992). Dr. Clawson is also the editor of *Strategic Assessment* (NDU Press), the annual Institute survey of U.S. Security challenges in the post-Cold War period. A past editor of *Orbis*, Dr. Clawson was a senior economist at the World Bank and the International Monetary Fund.

1. DEMOGRAPHIC STRESSES

Part I examined the great powers and the challenges they might pose to U.S. interests. Part II also examines potential sources of conflict: conflicts stemming from broad, environment-related stresses involving disturbances in the ecological balance between humanity and nature.

Society can be stressed by population growth but also by other population dynamics, such as the structure and distribution of population. To a demographer, population structure means the distribution of a given population by age and gender. Distribution refers to the spatial distribution of population, such as rural-urban or regional balance within a country or the movement of people among countries. This section examines three types of stresses: from population growth, from changing population structure (the bulge in working-age adults), and from population distribution (mass migration).

POPULATION GROWTH

The global rate of population growth is slowing and is likely to continue to slow for decades to come. Table 1 shows that the world's population grew 1.90 percent between 1954 and 1974, fell to 1.73 percent from 1974 to 1994 and is on track to fall further to 1.35 percent from 1994 to 2014. These data are from the U.S. Census Bureau; the estimates from the other two major sources of population data, the World Bank, and the United Nations Fund for Population Activities, are quite similar.[1]

The explanation for the declining rate of population growth is a fall off in birth rates. The number of children a woman will have during her lifetime is called the fertility rate. According to World Bank data, the global average fertility rate declined by one-third from 1970 to 1992: women formerly had 4.9 children on average, but only 3.1 by the end of the period. The fertility rate in the developed world fell from 2.4 to 1.7, below the replacement rate of 2.1-2.2. But there was also a systematic decline in fertility in developing countries in every part of the world. That decline started in the 1970s in East Asia, with remarkable declines in South Korea, Taiwan, China, Hong Kong, Singapore. It later spread to South Asia and Latin America. Middle East fertility rates plummeted quickly from the mid-1980s. Sub-Saharan African fertility rates have declined the least of any part of the world, but they too have fallen.

Table 1. World Population, 1954, 1974, 1994, 2014 and 2034, in millions

	1954	1974	1994	2014	2034
World	2,748	4,005	5,642	7,386	8,410
Increase in 20 years		1,257	1,637	1,744	1,024
Growth rate		1.90%	1.73%	1.35%	0.66%
Developed	877	1,084	1,240	1,350	1,024
Growth rate		1.07%	.67%	0.43%	-0.06%
Developing	1,872	2,921	4,402	6,036	7,070
Growth rate		2.25%	2.07%	1.59%	0.78%

Source: U.S. Bureau of the Census, World Population Profile: 1994. Data for 2014 interpolated from 2010 and 2020. Data for 2034 estimated using growth rates for 2025-2050 from World Bank, *World Population Projections 1994-95.*

This trend led to this conclusion:[2]

> The developing world is undergoing a reproductive revolution. . . . Recent evidence suggests that birth rates in the developing world have fallen even in the absence of improved living conditions. The decrease also proceeded with remarkable speed. Developing countries appear to have benefitted from the growing scope of family-planning programs, from new contraceptive technologies and from the educational power of mass media.

While the population growth rate has fallen, the absolute number of people being added each year to the world population is still increasing. As table 1 shows, the global population increased 1,637 million from 1974 to 1994 and it will increase 1,744 million from 1994 to 2014. The explanation is "demographic momentum"—the number of women entering child-bearing years is rising fast enough to offset the drop in the number of children per woman. The demographic momentum will continue in and beyond 2015. In the next 20 years, the number of births each year will grow only slowly, from about 130 million in 1994 to about 140 million in 2015. That slow growth will reflect the expected continuing decline in fertility rates, offset by the 20 percent increase in the number of women entering child-bearing years (from 51 million to 62 million).

If the falling population growth rate is the big news, the more often-told population story is the change in the distribution among regions. In the next 20 years, the share of the developed world in global population will decline from 22 to 18 percent. Of more interest, the generally midincome or high-growth developing regions will also see their share of world population decline, from 39 to 36 percent. The area that will increase its share in world population is the "poverty belt" that extends from Bangladesh west across the Middle East and south across Africa to the Cape of Good Hope. Its proportion of world population will increase from 39 percent in 1994 to 46 percent in 2015; it will account for 68 percent of world population growth during those 20 years.

Table 2. Fertility Rates, 1970 and 1992

	1970	1992
World	4.9	3.1
Developed	2.4	1.7
Developing	5.6	3.3
East Asia	5.7	2.3
South Asia	6.0	4.0
Middle East and Southwest Asia	6.8	4.9
Latin America	5.2	3.0
Sub-Saharan Africa	6.5	6.1

Source: World Bank, *World Development Report 1994*.

The change in the distribution of the world's population is, as such things go, quite dramatic. There is an intuitively appealing notion that those countries with more rapidly growing population will want to take resources away from those states with less rapidly growing population. However, the parts of the world with the most rapid population growth are generally the poorest areas with the least military might. That suggests the rapidly growing states are not well positioned to cause conventional military problems for the slow-growing states. Furthermore, the states with rapid population growth are grouped in one swath of the world, which means that only a few such states have borders with the slow population-growth states. The potential for conventional military conflict seems greatest along that border, which runs from the Indian Ocean along the eastern edge of India, across the southern edge of the former Soviet Union, and through the Mediterranean out to the Atlantic.

THE BULGE IN WORKING-AGE ADULTS

As a result of the rapid population growth in the last few decades plus the more recent slowdown in the rate of growth, the age structure of the world population is going to change over the next 20 years. Table 4 shows that the number of children is unlikely to experience significant growth. The number of those turning age 2 will go from 127 million in 1994 to 139 million in 2015, a growth of only 12 million or 9 percent. On the other hand, the number of elderly will be growing rapidly. Those turning age 67 numbered 27 million in 1994 but should be 45 million in 2015, an increase of 18 million or 67 percent. In absolute numbers, the largest growth will be in the age groups in their prime earning years, between the late teens and the mid fifties. For instance, those turning 52 will increase from 45 million in 1994 to about 77 million in 2015.

The effect of this change in age structure will be to create a much larger group of working-age adults. The International Labor Office (ILO) made an estimate of how this will change the world labor force, factoring in expected changes in the percent of men and women of working age who are in the labor force (what economists call the labor force participation rate). At first glance, it does not seem that the period 1995–2015 will be very different from the period 1974–1994: in the next 20 years, the world labor force will grow by 783 million, while in the last 20 years, it grew by 767 million. In other words, it looks like the increase in the number of the elderly will offset the increase in the number of young adults.

Table 3. Population by Region, 1994 and 2015

	(in millions)			(percent)		
	1994	2015	Change	1994	2015	Change
World	5,642	7,386	1,744	100.0%	100.0%	100.0%
Developed	1,240	1,350	110	22.0%	18.3%	6.3%
North America	289	342	53	5.1%	4.6%	3.0%
FSU	296	327	31	5.2%	4.4%	1.8%
Other Europe	509	529	20	9.0%	7.2%	1.1%
Japan, Australia, New Zealand	146	153	7	2.6%	2.1%	0.4%
Developing	4,402	6,036	1,634	78.0%	81.7%	93.6%
Generally Midincome or High Growth	2,172	2,622	450	38.5%	35.5%	25.9%
Latin America	474	613	139	8.4%	8.3%	8.0%
China	1,190	1,379	189	21.1%	18.7%	10.9%
Korea & Southeast Asia	508	630	122	9.0%	8.5%	7.0%
Generally Low Income or Low Growth	2,230	3,413	1,183	39.4%	46.2%	67.8%
South Asia and Southwest Asia	1,379	1,987	608	24.4%	26.9%	34.9%
Middle East	279	440	161	4.9%	6.0%	9.2%
Sub-Saharan Africa	572	986	414	10.1%	13.3%	23.7%

Source: U.S. Bureau of the Census, *World Population Profile: 1994*. Data for 2015 interpolated from 2010 and 2020. The Middle East is defined as the Arab states plus Israel.

But the picture changes sharply when we look at the numbers more closely. What we find is two groups of countries going very different ways. The first group is the developed world and China, in which the labor force is going to be growing slowly. In this group of countries, the population is aging: many people are retiring, and there are relatively few young adults because births fell off by the 1970s. The situation is entirely different in the second group of countries, i.e., the developing world outside of China. These countries are experiencing an explosion in the labor force. In the period 1950–1970, their labor force grew by 10 million people a year; in the period 1970–1990, their labor force grew by 20 million people a year; and in the period 1990–2010, it will grow by 30 million people a year. Over the 20-year period 1950-1970, that translates into 206 million; 1970–1990, 406 million; and 1990–2010, 604 million.

Table 4. Population at Various Ages, 1994 and 2015 (in millions)

	Population at Age:					
	2	10	17	32	52	67
1994						
World	127	116	103	85	45	27
Developed	17	18	17	19	14	10
Developing	110	98	86	66	31	17
2015						
World	139	123	124	107	77	45
Developed	16	17	17	18	17	14
Developing	123	116	107	89	60	31
Change 1994-2015 for the World::						
In absolute numbers	12	7	21	22	32	18
In Percent	9%	6%	20%	26%	71%	67%

Source: U.S. Bureau of the Census, *World Population Profile: 1994*. Data for 2015 interpolated from 2000 and 2020. Estimated from data on population aged 0-4, 5-14, 15-19, 20-44, 45-59, and 60-74.

The developing world outside of China is unlikely to be able to create sufficient jobs to absorb the 30 million people joining the labor force each year. Keeping up with the labor force growth was difficult enough in the period 1950–1970, when there were only 10 million new workers a year and when the world economy was expanding at a rapid rate. In the period 1970–1990, as the world economy (outside of East Asia) slowed and as the number of new workers rose steeply, unemployment and underemployment grew.

Perhaps an increase in unemployment and underemployment in the period 1990–2010 can be avoided, if world economic activity grows more rapidly, if developed countries permit more imports of labor-intensive products like garments, and if developing country governments adopt policies to promote job creation (for instance, encouraging labor-intensive industries instead of showcase, capital-intensive projects). However, the most likely prospect for the next 20 years is a substantial increase in those looking in vain for productive employment in the developing world outside of China. Many of these people will fill their time with peddling or offering to do odd jobs. They may not be unemployed in a strict sense, but they will be so severely underemployed, at such a low-income level relative to their potential, that they might as well be considered unemployed.

Table 5. World Labor Force, 1950-2030 (in millions)

	1950	1970	1990	2010	2030
World	1,189	1,597	2,364	3,147	3,740
Developed	387	477	586	636	620
Developing	802	1,120	1,778	2,511	3,120
China	317	428	680	809	780
Other	485	691	1,098	1,702	2,340

Growth over 20 Years

	1950	1970	1990	2010	2030
World		408	767	783	593
Developed		90	109	50	-16
Developing		317	658	733	609
China		111	252	129	-29
Other		206	406	604	638

Source: International Labor Office, *Economically Active Population Estimates and Projections 1950-2025* (Geneva, 1986). 2030 estimated from data for 2025.

The problem of unemployment and underemployment is likely to be concentrated among young adults, unable to get a start in the working world, rather than among middle-aged or older workers (layoffs of older workers has been rather uncommon in the developing world). Unemployed young adults can pose a serious political problem, because this is the group with the fewest ties to the established order (e.g., fewer family obligations) and most sympathetic to idealistic political radicalism. An example of this problem can be seen in the violence in Algeria, which has its roots as much in youth unemployment as in any religious fervor. Under the base-case scenario, in the developing world outside of China we can expect an increase in domestic political violence from underemployed youths under the influence of radical extremists.

In those developing countries where the bulge in the working-age population is put to effective use, the economic future is bright. The demographic transition offers an opening for rapid growth during the generation when the proportion of those in the labor force is at a record high—the proportion of children have fallen, while the share of the elderly in the population has not yet risen. Demography makes use of the concept of the dependency ratio, that is, the ratio of the population not in the labor force to the population in the labor force. China, which is in the midst of the demographic period favorable to growth, has a dependency ratio of 0.66 (463 million not in the labor force; 699 millon in it), according to the World Bank (*World Development Report 1994*; data for 1992). Sub-Saharan Africa has a dependency ratio of 1.45 (321 million not in the labor force; 222 million in it). That means every three people in the Chinese labor force support two dependents, while every three Africans in the labor force support four dependents. That difference explains part of the reason that China's economic growth rate has been more rapid than Africa's. In 2015, numerous developing countries will be in the favorable demographic situation China now enjoys. Some of these developing countries may be able to make effective use of the opportunity provided by the low dependency ratio.

Turning from the working-age population to the elderly, the immediate effect of the fall in the fertility rate can be positive. The elderly can do very well, because their adult children with few children of their own can readily afford to support their parents. This phenomenon is quite common in contemporary China. By 2015, China will face a new demographic situation, which other developing countries will reach some decades later: the elderly will be such a significant proportion of the population that they will have to sustain themselves from their own savings, rather than relying on support from their adult children. Generating those savings will be a major challenge. If sufficient savings can be set aside now, investment funds will permit more rapid job growth now and will generate earnings that can sustain the elderly later. On the other hand, a savings shortfall could lead to unrest later as the elderly's needs place a heavier and heavier burden on society. China, the developing country now facing most acutely this savings challenge, has risen to the occasion. Numerous other developing countries—e.g., much of Latin America—will by 2015 be in the situation China is in today. It is not clear if they will have the same success China has had at generating the necessary savings to create jobs and to provide for the elderly later.

These forecasts about world population are based on the consensus forecast of the impact of AIDS and other global epidemics. If in fact the incidence of such epidemics is greater than expected, the effect would be to reduce the population growth rate faster than expected, which would reduce population pressures even more rapidly than in the base case considered here. Those most likely to die would be the young, especially infants, though that may be somewhat less true for AIDS than for other epidemics. However, in the developing world, AIDS kills primarily infants affected at birth and sexually active young adults, who die in their thirties. Epidemics also affect the elderly, but the greatest expected impact of epidemics would be in the countries with the poorest medical systems, where the elderly form a small part of the population. Because those who die in epidemics are most likely to be the young, the share of the elderly in the world population would probably be greater than in the base case. The effect on the labor force is not as clear. To the extent that future epidemics kill the retired elderly, they would not affect the labor force at all; to the extent they kill infants, they would not affect the labor force until after 2015; but to the extent that they kill the sexually active young, they would reduce the labor force immediately.

MIGRATION

One important aspect of international migration is and will continue to be the steady movement of people seeking a better life abroad. The number of such migrants is likely to grow for various reasons. Borders are becoming more porous because of the spread of liberal values like freedom of movement; few governments have the tight control on foreign travel common to the old communist bloc. Technological advances are making communication and transportation easier and cheaper. Migrant communities in host countries develop social networks across borders, creating a social infrastructure for further migration. Migrants are driven by the deterioration in economic circumstances in the unsuccessful states and by the increasing disparity between the unsuccessful and the successful economies. Furthermore, political unrest is becoming more common in unsuccessful states, from the fringes of the old Soviet empire to sub-Saharan Africa.

While such migrant flows are undoubtedly an important social problem, it is not obvious that the U.S. military will be asked to play a major role in responding to that problem. Consider the migrant flow into the United States. A large part of the flow into the United States is by legal migrants, for which there is no military role. The most likely area for a military role is guarding the border from illegal crossings, more of a police function than a conventional military role, especially since it is unlikely that those crossing the border will use weapons (other than sidearms and the occasional rifle) to fend off those patrolling the borders. Since World War II, quasipolice functions have been rarely performed by the U.S. military, other than by the Coast Guard and the National Guard.

The most likely role for the U.S. military is in responding to refugee problems, especially sudden waves of refugees. These waves can produce humanitarian disasters that are brought to the world's attention by television coverage that emphasizes horrific images. It is instructive that those conflicts that cannot be covered by television, such as the conflict in southern Sudan, receive less attention from policy makers than do those from which pictures are beamed into our living rooms. Policy makers, leery of intervention, can find themselves forced by television-generated public pressure to send in military units. In other words, the U.S. military may be asked to respond to refugee waves anywhere in the world.

Such mass exoduses will occur more often for several reasons:

❏ Better communication allows large groups to learn quickly of impending political troubles, and therefore to flee at about the same time.

❏ From experiences like those of Hutus in Rwanda fleeing to Zaire or the Kurds in Iraq fleeing to Turkey, people the world over have learned that mass movements are a good way to get the world's attention and to overwhelm controls in the destination countries.

❏ Some governments will provoke refugee flows.[3] Assaults on the food supply have been a key military strategy in some African conflicts as a means to deprive rebel movements of recruits and to force the exodus of civilians from the conflict zone. The threat of causing a refugee outflow can be used as a bargaining chip to secure economic aid or political concessions from the likely destination countries or the international community. Refugees can be used to assert de facto control over the areas to where they move (e.g., across the border into a neighboring country).

❏ Some governments will welcome refugee inflows. The presence of famine has brought international relief, the diversion of which became a key source for financing wars in Ethiopia, Somalia, Sudan, and Mozambique.

❏ Some rebel groups will encourage refugee departures at times. Refugee camps provide fertile grounds for their propaganda and for recruiting soldiers. Refugee camps can also serve as useful base camps for "refugee warriors," providing safe areas for recuperation and training as well as a potential logistics center.

Sources of Migrants

Over the past two decades there has been an alarming increase in refugees in the world. The total rose from 2.8 million in 1976, to 8.6 million in 1980 to over 19 million in 1994. According to the United Nations High Commissioner for Refugees (UNHCR), during 1994 an average of 10,000 people a day became refugees, even using the narrow definition of refugee contained in the 1951 U.N. Refugee Convention. The number of refugees is likely to grow.

While the risks of future East-West refugee movements are considerable, most migration experts believe that, in the long term, migratory pressure to the North from the South will be far stronger than from the East. Most future refugee movements will occur either as a result of demands for democratization in many parts of the developing and post-Communist worlds or as a result of the communal violence and the fragmentation of existing states caused by nationality disputes and ethnic and religious conflicts. Political upheavals in unstable regions will be exacerbated by the diffusion of weapons via the arms trade from the advanced to the developing world.

Middle East. European policy makers in particular are concerned that large-scale immigration from North Africa and the Middle East will have dangerous social and political consequences. Opposition to migrants is a major feature of contemporary European politics. To many Europeans the presence of large Islamic communities raises key questions about nationality and cultural pluralism. Fear of Islamic fundamentalism and terrorism, increasing violence between migrants and local populations, and the growing popularity of extremist right-wing, anti-immigrant political parties are impeding the assimilation of the millions of Muslim migrants and their families now living in Western Europe. In 1950, Muslim refugees represented only 12 percent of the world's refugee population. In 1970, they made up 50 percent. In 1990, almost 75 percent of the world's refugees were Muslim. Given the likely future increase in the number of Islamic Fundamentalist movements both in the former Soviet Union and elsewhere, the total number of Muslim refugees could represent well over 90 percent of the world's forcibly displaced people by the end of first decade of the 21st century. Future domestic and regional instability in the Middle East is also likely to generate new flows of refugees to neighboring countries and Europe. Most regimes in the region lack legitimacy and are moving toward domestic crises as they fail to meet popular demands for improved economic and social conditions or pressures for more political participation. Future political change in the region will in turn provoke major social change as old elites lose their grip on power and are forced to give way to new groups, including ethnic and religious minorities. Political changes of this kind usually produce large refugee movements consisting of entire classes of people who are linked to the old order.

Western Hemisphere. Several countries have the potential to expel refugees or to generate forced migrants. Haiti and Cuba present the gravest risk of uncontrolled mass movements to the United States in the near future. However, the United States, with the highest standard of living in the Western Hemisphere and a tradition of political freedom, will draw many aliens from all over the world to its borders.

China. The increased smuggling of Chinese nationals into the United States by international criminal rings is perhaps the most dramatic example of the global "pull" of the United States. Continued Chinese emigration in the years ahead is extremely likely given the political instability and the breakdown of central control that will probably occur in China after the death of Deng Xiaoping. Dramatic economic and social change in

China is already spurring an annual exodus of tens of thousands of Chinese seeking opportunity or political freedom abroad. China's internal migrant population, made up mainly of unemployed peasants, has grown to more than 100 million and is increasing by perhaps 13 million a year. If these internal migrants are unable to find employment, they will look to emigration as an increasingly attractive and viable option. Indeed, the Chinese government will come to see out-migration as a safety valve against overpopulation, unemployment and internal migration from the countryside to the cities.

Africa. Even if democratization succeeds in Africa, it does not mean that there will be an end to ethnic conflicts and refugee movements. Indeed, democratization may in fact be destabilizing—especially if the process of liberalization gives free rein to demands from national minorities for greater autonomy or secession. Thus, it is likely that with the end or weakening of authoritarian regimes across Africa, long-repressed factional grievances and antagonisms will result in increased conflicts as groups contend for control of the political systems.

Absorption

Migration has always been a major component in U.S. population growth, and it has in this century become an important factor in the population growth of most northern European countries. The willingness, if not eagerness, of these countries to accept a continuing flow of migrants is not likely to change. The southern European countries are in the process of becoming significant destinations for migration, leaving Japan as the odd man out among the industrial countries in attitude towards migration.

In the last 20 years, developing countries have been host to most of the world's refugees; indeed, they have been the largest recipients of migrants as a whole. That is primarily a function of proximity to the migrant and refugee sources. For instance, when 50,000 Tadzhik refugees fled to Afghanistan during the Tadzhik civil war in autumn 1992, that was not because of a strong desire to live in Afghanistan. Because Africa and the Middle East are likely to continue to be the sources of most of the world's migrants and refugees, their countries are also likely to continue to host most of the world's migrants and refugees. An important political and social issue will be whether the large number of Chinese now on the move will start heading into the traditional countries of Chinese emigration in Southeast Asia, which could create both social and political tensions in countries with important Chinese business communities that hold little political power at present (e.g., Indonesia, Malaysia, Thailand, and Vietnam).

The willingness of the host countries to absorb migrants is likely to fall significantly short of the demand for spaces, and the demand is likely to rise. At the same time, unemployment problems in the industrial nations are likely to continue for at least another decade under the most optimistic scenarios, while in the developing world, job creation will probably fall significantly short of need.

This gap between migrant demand for reception and industrial country willingness to supply space will pose a particular problem in the event of a sudden refugee exodus. In theory, most countries have accepted the obligation to permit entry without limit to those fleeing a well-founded fear of persecution in their home country and to allow temporary residence until the danger of persecution at home passes. In practice, this right was aimed at refugees from Communist lands and only applied to others as convenient (e.g., by Somalia's government in the 1970s and 1980s to ethnic Somalis from Ethiopia). With the end of the Cold War, the right to asylum has been significantly eroded and is not likely to be restored. European nations have used a variety of mechanisms to prevent granting asylum to those fleeing what is obviously a well-grounded fear of persecution in the former Yugoslavia. The United States has adopted much stricter regulations with regard to asylum-seekers from Haiti and Cuba, among others.

In theory, refugees are temporary and will be repatriated eventually. That in fact does happen to significant numbers of refugees to developing countries, who are less prone to integrate themselves into their host societies than are those who are accorded asylum in industrial nations. In 1992, 2.4 million refugees returned home, including 1.5 million to Afghanistan and 178,000 to Mozambique. Repatriation is generally voluntary; forcible repatriation, as with Vietnamese boat people in the late 1980s and Haitians in 1994, has been on a smaller scale. Increasing the return flow involves providing logistical assistance for the move, setting up on-site reception centers at the resettlement locations, and furnishing help in reintegrating refugees. It may also require a continuing international military presence to protect returnees from violence and persecution.

Intervention

While the United States does not have a security interest (narrowly defined) in responding to every refugee exodus or the situation that provoked it, the suffering offends our values, and therefore Washington is likely to provide aid. Furthermore, American public opinion tolerates poorly a selective policy of responding to only some refugee disasters. The lack of response in April and May 1994 to the slaughters in Rwanda raised concerns that the United States was being less sensitive to the death of blacks than it would have been to the death of those of other races. In the end, the United States and the world community found themselves compelled to intervene in Rwanda, having to use a larger force than might have been necessary had action been taken earlier. Based in part on this experience, the United States and the international community are moving towards a consensus that the world's governments have an obligation to provide relief in every humanitarian disaster, including refugee mass exoduses and even civil wars.

None of the options for dealing with refugee flows is attractive:

❑ Forceful interception sits poorly with the U.S. self-image as a land of refuge and as open country. Even when interception commands widespread popular support, as in the summer 1994 Haitian and Cuban cases, the action is on the front pages of the newspapers and generates challenge in the courts.

❑ Providing permanent resettlement is not practical given the reluctance to accept large numbers of immigrants, as well as the experience with Vietnamese boat refugees which demonstrates that resettlement encourages more refugees.

❑ Temporary asylum is not popular in industrial countries because of concerns that refugees will stay for the long term, as seen in European reactions to the refugees from the former Yugoslavia.

❑ Establishing refugee camps in border zones is a race against death, as so tragically demonstrated by the Rwandan refugees in Zaire.

❑ Dealing with the problem of displacement in the country of origin requires a presence in failed states, which runs the risk of escalating into intervention into a civil war. Examples of steps to be taken are: helping to provide assistance to victims of ethnic conflict as close to their homes as possible, creating havens or secure areas where displaced persons can get help in relative safety, deploying troops to prevent the expulsions of civilians in some areas, and protecting relief workers who are caught in the cross-fire between opposing sides.

In many cases, the most successful approach is likely to be the last, that is, resolving the crisis provoking people to want to leave. A recent Trilateral Commission study concluded, "A broad consensus is developing in Trilateral countries [North America, Western Europe, and Japan] that receiving countries must be attentive to pre-refugee, pre-migration circumstances in sending countries. Conflict prevention and other political and assistance initiatives must be mobilized quickly and early to prevent them from becoming crises."[4] The early intervention may be combined with bottling up the refugee flow in the interim, as was done in the Haitian case. The bottling-up approach, as important as it may be in the short run, is unlikely to be successful in the long run unless the underlying crisis ends. After all, not even the Berlin Wall worked in the end.

The problem is how to take sufficient measures to end the crisis provoking the refugee flight without having to become involved in resolving all the deep-rooted conflicts in a failed state. If too little is done, the military and the relief agencies can be bogged down in protracted humanitarian operations. If too much is attempted, the military can be perceived by one side to have intervened in a civil war on behalf of its enemies. That in turn can lead to taking casualties and a loss of U.S. public support for the intervention.

While the principal responsibility for responding to mass refugee exoduses will continue to fall to non-governmental organizations supplemented by the office of the U.N. High Commissioner on Refugees and the U.S. Office of Foreign Disaster Assistance, the U.S. military will be called upon repeatedly. It has instant access to a range of material and logistical resources in transportation, communications and medical services which are simply not available to humanitarian organizations. That said, the military is not likely to be the first choice in responding to mass refugee exoduses or similar disasters. The consensus view appears to be, "Military assets should be employed in a humanitarian emergency intervention only when they have a comparative advantage over other relief organizations."[5]

2. POLLUTION AND RESOURCE STRESSES

GLOBAL POLLUTION

In recent decades the world has increasingly been beset by global environmental problems that involve the use and management of global common property like the oceans and the atmosphere that are in some sense owned collectively by all nations rather than being the sovereign territory of any single nation. From this common territory, valuable resources can be harvested or extracted, and this common territory is often used as a repository for waste. As is typical with a resource available without charge, the "global commons" has been overused without adequate concern for its long-term maintenance. Concern about misuse has focused on chloroflourocarbons (CFCs), global warming, and acid rain. These and other concerns are unlikely to disappear over the next 20 years.

The problems of the global commons often involve intangible values, such as some kinds of environmental or ecological stress, as distinct from tangible, priced resources. This is not a legitimate conceptual distinction to economists, who would argue for recognizing the economic cost of air or water pollution no less than the cost of buying fuels and investing in equipment to generate electricity. But the pathways by which economic activity generate environmental damage are in many cases still mired in scientific uncertainty; certainly no money value can be assigned to damages. ("Let's see you prove that China is responsible for acid rain over Japan" or "Show me that building this or that dam will seriously disrupt the flyway of migrating bird species.") Thus, for genuine or disingenuous reasons, it is easy to obstruct settlement of global environmental disputes.

Because the "service" provided by the global commons (like clean air) is outside the market system, there is little prospect that global environmental conflicts will be resolved through price adjustment or other automatic market measures, of the sort that can do so much to resolve shortages of raw materials. Similarly, unilateral national regulatory action is unlikely to be helpful, since in most cases the essential problem is beyond the regulatory reach of any single country. The major action likely to be effective in dealing with global environmental problems almost surely will be international agreements, not any application of military force or any threat to use military force.

The ozone problem shows what can be done to resolve such problems. CFCs are chemical compounds with wide application in aerosol propellants, coolants in refrigeration and air conditioning, foam-blowing agents, and solvents for cleaning electrical compounds. In the 1970s, scientific evidence began to mount that these compounds, long thought to be benign, could cause depletion of the stratospheric ozone layer which shields the earth from damaging ultraviolet radiation. As a result, in 1987, the Montreal Protocol on Substances that Deplete the Ozone Layer was signed by 24 countries. There have been some implementation problems, such as India's unwillingness to cooperate. Nevertheless, this was a model case for a global environmental problem that can be easily resolved because: (1) the damages were identified and generally accepted as serious by the scientific community; (2) the negative effects would be expected to be experienced by all countries (all losers, no gainers); (3) the cost of resolving the problem (phasing out CFCs), while substantial, was not prohibitive; and (4) the firms producing the offending product were able to develop alternatives that allowed them to preserve their profits.

The global warming problem, said to be caused by the buildup of carbon into he atmosphere, is in some respects similar to the ozone problem, but with a less ready solution. The scientific evidence is more ambiguous. Some countries may experience a beneficial climate change from global warming; it is not clear who would be the gainers and who the losers, nor how much they would gain or lose. The costs of mitigating carbon buildup in the atmosphere can potentially be very high, since it could require reductions in fossil-fuel burning. For all these reasons, it is not surprising that the only international accord on global warming—the 1992 Framework Convention on Climate Change—is vague and experiencing significant problems in implementation.

Much like global pollution problems, regional pollution issues are also most likely to be addressed through international agreements. Not without fits and starts, and with a fair amount of contentiousness, the 12-member European Community (now European Union) has progressed far in adopting timetables and standards for controlling SO_2 and NOx releases from power plants and other combustion facilities. Acidification of Scandinavian lakes and forest decay in Germany's almost mythically venerated Black Forest are among the more publicized examples of the damage believed to be brought about by these gases. Consensus on mitigation was no doubt helped by the fact that most of the EU member countries are economically well off and so are inclined to accord environmental remediation a relatively high priority. But just as important, at least in Western Europe, is the fact that these emissions are significant sources of both internal and external pollution. Internally, this helps ensure domestic political support for adopting abatement policies and meeting their cost. Externally, the ubiquitousness of pollution creates a kind of "mutually assured (environmental) destruction" evoking a degree of cooperation that might not prevail under different circumstances.

There is considerable potential for conflict among states about how to address global environmental problems. There are at least two kinds of situations in which some countries may be unwilling to cooperate. The simple case is the that of the "free rider." A country may recognize that something should be done about a particular problem, but chose not to do what it may acknowledge (in private) is its fair share, believing that even if it does not participate, the other countries will satisfactorily address the problem and the non-cooperating country will benefit, without incurring any costs. The more complex case occurs when a country believes that the global community is willing to induce their cooperation with various types of payoffs. For example, some East European countries may expect that the developed world will provide the resources required to reduce carbon emissions.

RESOURCE SHORTAGES

Twenty years ago, in 1975, security analysts were concerned about the world running out of energy, minerals, and foodstuffs, all of which were at record-high prices. Twenty years before that, in 1955, analysts were concerned that the United States was becoming dependent on foreign sources for strategic minerals. Neither of these concerns turned out to be justified; neither of the issues that so absorbed analysts came to be problems 20 years later on. The principal lesson should be caution about how well we can forecast. That said, let us look at what seems to be the most reasonable forecast based on the information now available.

Minerals and Agricultural Products

The conventional wisdom is that the world is running out of many natural resources and that in the future it will be more difficult to obtain the mineral and agricultural products necessary for the continuation of economic development.[6] By contrast, in the view of most economists, the evidence suggests that mineral and agricultural products are if anything becoming more readily available. Economists look at the real (inflation-adjusted) price as the best measure of economic availability or scarcity. A rising real price indicates growing economic scarcity while a declining real price indicates increasing relative availability. In studies by Potter and Christy, updated by Manthy, the long-term inflation-adjusted price trends for a whole series of mineral and agricultural products were found to be stable and declining, with a few exceptions (notably lumber and fish). The graph of prices of oil in 1967 dollars per barrel and of corn in 1967 dollars per bushel illustrates this

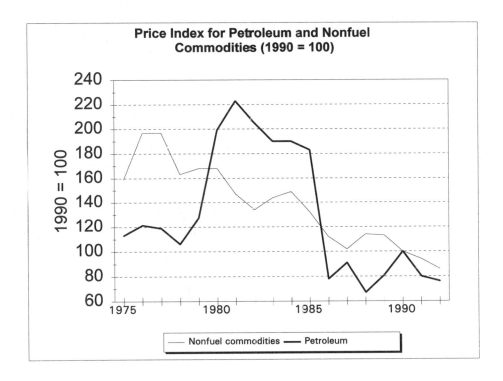

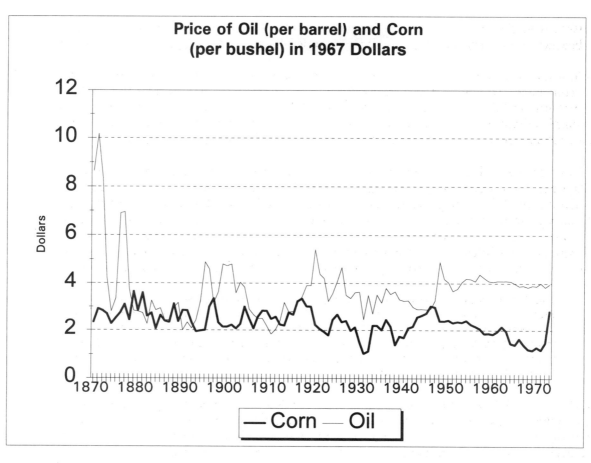

Price of Oil (per barrel) and Corn (per bushel) in 1967 Dollars

— Corn — Oil

flat or slightly declining character of commodity prices (oil is the line on top, with higher spikes and lower valleys).

During the 1970s, many argued that the period of stable mineral and agricultural prices was being replaced by an increasing resource scarcity as reflected in the rising real prices for a broad range of products, not just for petroleum. However, any belief that the pattern of the 1970s was permanent was shattered by the price pattern of the 1980s, during which the price of resource-based commodities declined and then stabilized at or below the levels that prevailed in the 1950s and 1960s. Indeed, World Bank data in the graph below show that the period 1985–1992 was characterized by ample supply conditions for many raw materials with historic low prices and unused capacity in many agricultural and mineral products. It would be unwise to assume this trend will persist. It is more appropriate to read the last 30 years as a period of high variance around stable prices, with 5 years of very high prices (1973-1978) and 10 years of relatively low prices (1985-1994).

The explanation for the long-term price stability of most mineral and agricultural products is probably found in the effect of technology on production costs. New production techniques allow: (1) use of what previously would have been discarded as waste; e.g., wood processing now utilizes a greater portion of each log and foresters harvest tree species that once were left to rot or burn; (2) exploitation of reserves that would have previously been uneconomical to exploit, e.g., in petroleum, oil fields found at greater depths or offshore in deeper water, plus fields in which the oil is at low pressure or too viscous to flow readily. In some sense the global situation can be viewed as a race between technology and demand. Over the past 200 years, technology has been winning.

In addition, higher prices for a certain specific raw material in certain periods generate economic incentives for the development of products that use less of that raw material, perhaps by substituting other raw materials. When one commodity comes into short supply, there is a natural shift to use others. For instance, fiber optics that utilize abundant resources for making glass are replacing scarce and expensive copper.

The trend for stable commodity prices in the last 200 years is a fact of history. This does not mean the trend will persist for the next 20 years; the record is full of forecasts of sudden shifts. There appears little reason to expect a shift in the fundamental balance that has allowed for the expansion of raw material use without increased real resource prices, however. Indeed, population growth is slowing, which should reduce the rate of expansion of raw material demand. A reasonable judgment for the world is that of the Resources for the Future study team, writing in 1964 about the prospects for the U.S. to 2000:[7]

> The rest of the twentieth century affords the prospect of sustained economic growth in the United States supported by adequacy of resource materials—*provided* technological advances and economic adaptation continue, *provided* foreign sources of raw materials remain open through maintenance of a viable world trading system, and *provided* government resource policies and private management of resource enterprises improve in farsightedness, flexibility and consistency.

One might ask what type of warning would we have of an increasing long-term global scarcity for resource-based raw materials. A critical signal would be rising real prices. However, short-term price rises need not necessarily be disturbing, for raw material prices typically rise during a business boom and fall during a recession. However, should a real price rise persist, this could be indicative of growing relative long-term scarcity.

Of all commodities about a shortage of which we may worry, oil may be most troubling for several reasons. One is the high value of world oil trade: $200 billion per annum, equal to 5 percent of the world's exports of goods and services (though it is less than 1 percent of the world's GDP). Another is that nearly half of all oil produced in the world is exported from one country to another, unlike most commodities for which there is a large reserve of production that could be diverted if needed to meet a shortage in the international trade circuits. A third factor, perhaps the most important, is that oil production is highly concentrated in one region, and a politically unstable one at that. In 1994, the Persian Gulf provided 25 percent of world oil output. Furthermore, if the price of oil stays low, as seems most likely, then dependence on Persian Gulf oil will increase, because it is the lowest cost oil to produce. Ashland Oil forecasts that in 2010, world oil demand will be 76 to 87 million barrels per day (mbd), compared to million in 1994.[8] Non-Persian Gulf producers could, Ashland estimates, provide 47 to 57 mbd of that demand. In the event that world oil demand rises at the high end of the estimate and non-Gulf production remains at the low end, then the Gulf could be called upon to supply 40 mbd out of a world demand of 87 mbd. Such a high level of dependence on one region, and especially on Saudi Arabia, would make the world economy vulnerable to political shocks in the Gulf.

Note that the issue is not one of the world running out of oil, but instead of an increasing concentration on supply from one region. Consider that world oil reserves in 1994 were about 1,000 billion barrels. The practice in the best-run U.S. fields is to produce each year about 7 percent of reserves, which if done on a worldwide, would imply a production capacity of 190 mbd, more than twice the expected 2010 demand (Persian Gulf producers prefer to produce at a much lower rate in order to keep supply limited and prices high). And reserves have a way of increasing. Consider that in 1937, world proved oil reserves were 40 billion barrels; in 1960, 300 billion barrels;[9] in 1994, 1,000 billion barrels. The demand-to-reserve ratio has been roughly constant for 60 years.

So much for the 1970s concern about raw material scarcity worldwide. What about the 1950s worry about the safety of supply for imported raw materials? The high degree of development and integration of the world's raw material markets suggest that, under most circumstances, countries can have ready access to raw materials through markets: imports suffice if local production is low. The open global trading system is widening to incorporate more and more states, and it is deepening through development of institutions (like the World Trade Organization) and agreements that guarantee more and more openness.

Given that many important materials are found throughout the globe and are being sold by many producers on well-established world markets, individual countries have limited ability to disrupt the world market for most raw materials, especially over longer time periods. For example, the Organization of Petroleum Exporting Countries (OPEC) has seen its market power erode substantially since the mid-1980s as a result of dissension among its members and development of alternative suppliers. Thus, although petroleum resources are vital to modern economies, the control of petroleum reserves is by no means a necessary or sufficient condition for either economic prosperity or national security. The presence of well-developed international petroleum markets allows any country access to the commodity, even during times of conflict.

Many economists have argued that the most cost-effective way for the U.S. to deal with the risk of petroleum disruption is through the promotion of increased private and public inventory stocks. The role for the government would be to both create its own strategic reserves and to establish incentives for private stocking. These stocks would reduce the need to intervene with force in order to ensure the flow of oil during a crisis; the stock would provide a flow during the months when alternative energy sources are brought into play (shifting electricity generation from oil to coal in dual-fuel-capable boilers, bringing into production oil wells temporarily not in use, etc.). Indeed, this stocking strategy is that adopted by the U.S. government, including the Strategic Petroleum Reserve, and by the industrial countries as a whole acting through the International Energy Agency (IEA). IEA members are pledged to maintain petroleum stockpiles equal to six months' imports.

Some countries are still worried about dependence on world markets for vital goods. A number of states argue that they need self-sufficiency in key foods, e.g., Japan with regard to rice. Such economic ignorance is politically harmless if it leads countries to waste their money on subsidizing domestic production of the supposedly vital commodity. But there is an important and politically troubling case. China has gone from being a petroleum exporter to being a petroleum importer. Given its economic growth rates and its vigorous steps since 1993 to promote automobile ownership by private individuals (which could lead to 25 million more cars by 2015), China is likely to import at least 2 mbd in 2015, even if it develops the oil fields in its isolated interior regions. China's current government does not seem to be fully comfortable with dependence on world markets for a vital input and may therefore seek a political alliance with an oil exporting state or states, on the expectation this would provide China with a more secure source of oil. The problem from the U.S. perspective is that China would probably decide that it could not make such a political alliance with the oil producers who are closely linked to the United States. China's most likely partners are the Middle East rogue states of Iran, Iraq, and Libya. Any such alliance could give these states access to some of China's advanced armaments. The most worrying scenario would be if the rogue states were able to take aggressive actions while under some sort of a Chinese nuclear umbrella (least plausibly, nuclear weapons sold to them by China; more plausibly, an implicit Chinese threat that an attack on the rogue states would draw a Chinese reaction).

The Natural Resource Base

A major concern today is the degradation of the globe's natural resource base, such as cultivable land and tropical forests. A related issue is the irreplaceable loss of biodiversity as species and local crop types become extinct.

The degradation of the natural resource base seems to occur during the early stages of industrialization and urbanization but to be reversed at a later stage of development. This V-curve can be seen clearly in the U.S. experience. In the United States during the 19th century, there was a sharp reduction in forested area, a depletion of soils from planting of marginal areas, and a conversion of rangeland into wastes because of overgrazing.[10] By contrast, in the last several decades, the quality of the natural environment in the United States has been on the upswing. A survey of renewable resources such as croplands, rangelands, forests, water, and wildlife, concluded:[11]

> Some valuable soil and water resources have for practical purposes been permanently depleted or degraded, and wetlands continue to be lost. In some cases, the introduction of new technologies has contributed to the decline and degradation of resources. Nevertheless, many of the earlier concerns over the demise of our renewable resources have faded. Threats of impending timber famine are now seldom heard. Typhoid epidemics from contaminated water supplies are a distant memory. In addition, many wildlife populations have recovered from the depths reached earlier in this century. Aquatic systems, forests, wildlife, rangeland, and cropland have demonstrated a remarkable capacity to restore themselves either naturally or in combination with sound management, once abuse and exploitative uses are reduced.

In addition to the economic issue of the natural resource base, there is the question of values: i.e., what priorities to accord the environment. The judgment of 1960 forecasting to the year 2000 seems appropriate for 1995 forecasting to 2015:[12]

> In contrast to the supply of resource materials, where problems will be the exception rather than rule, maintaining and improving the quality of land and water resources will be of increasing concern. Broadly speaking, this question of the natural environment is one of pleasant surroundings, although health and comfort are also involved.

Each year, the center of U.S. public opinion gives more weight to pleasant surroundings, partly because rising income creates more demand for such luxuries and partly because of changing attitudes. Indeed, the view that wildlife has as much right as humans has gone in the U.S. from being a fringe radical notion to being at the edge of the mainstream, and it is likely to become more acceptable in the future. That implies more priority for wildlife relative to humans. For instance, the major increase in the demand for water in the U.S. is for environmental purposes, such as letting fish thrive, rather than for human consumption. It is unlikely that the priorities on this matter in the United States (and to a lesser extent Europe) will be shared in most developing countries, where economic development is seen as more important by most of the population.

If the United States decides that there exists a serious problem in the deterioration of the world's natural resource base and in a loss of global biodiversity, the most likely remedial steps would be the same as in the case of global pollution, that is, international agreements. It is difficult to identify ways in which the U.S. military would become involved in addressing the problem, other than in monitoring and information collection about the global environment as a byproduct of the military's on-going intelligence collection (e.g., from satellites). In theory, the military could be asked to enforce international agreements, e.g., those protecting endangered whales. However, any such use of military force could erode international support for the underlying agreement, thereby becoming counterproductive.

TRANSBORDER RESOURCES

Some resources such as water naturally cross state borders. Water supplies naturally flow from one location to another, and water evaporates from lakes and streams in one country and falls back to earth as rain in another country. Water supplies are therefore fugitive resources that belong to no one until captured or withdrawn for use. For this reason, it is difficult to establish clear property rights over such resources. When ownership is established only by use, individuals as well as countries have an incentive to use the resource before it moves beyond their grasp or jurisdiction. In such circumstances, some of the costs of using water are imposed on other potential users within the hydrologic region in the form of diminished water quantity and quality.

About 200 river basins are shared by two or more countries. Thirteen are shared by five or more countries, and four—the Congo, Danube, Nile, and Niger—are shared by nine or more countries. Shared watersheds comprise about 47 percent of the global land area and more than 60 percent of the area on the continents of Africa, Asia, and South America. Groundwater resources are also frequently shared by two or more countries. Some river basins in which water conflict exists are the Euphrates, Jordan, Nile, Ganges, and Mekong.[13]

The development of markets and market-based prices provides for the peaceful transfer of most resources among countries. Under some very restrictive conditions, markets lead to an efficient distribution and use of a resource. And under a wide range of conditions, the market process contributes to a more efficient allocation and management of these resources. Markets can provide individual people as well as countries with increased opportunities and incentives to develop, transfer, and use a resource in ways that would benefit all parties. Two conditions must be satisfied for the development of efficient markets. There must be well-defined and transferable property rights in the resource being transferred and the full benefits and costs of the transfer must be borne by the buyers and sellers. Both conditions are likely to be violated for water resources. The fugitive nature of the resource makes it difficult to establish clear property rights, and the interdependencies among users make it likely that external factors or third-party impacts will result when the use or location of the water is changed.

The lack of clear property rights to international water resources is an obstacle to more efficient resource management and to the resolution of water conflicts. Property rights establish the initial conditions from which different parties can then negotiate to improve their positions. International law provides two opposing doctrines relating to property rights over international waters. The doctrine of *unlimited territorial sovereignty* states that a country has exclusive rights to the use of waters within its territory. This doctrine allows a country to deplete and pollute with no obligation to compensate adversely-affected parties. The contrasting doctrine of *unlimited territorial integrity* states that one country cannot alter the quantity and quality of water available to another. This doctrine greatly constrains how the upstream country can use the resource. In the absence of bargaining, both of these doctrines are likely to lead to inefficient outcomes. For example, under the first doctrine a country depleting or contaminating a shared resource has no incentive to mitigate the impact on the other countries regardless of the relative magnitude of the damages imposed and the costs of abatement. On the other hand, under the second doctrine the polluting country would have to mitigate all impacts regardless of how high the costs of mitigation and how small the impacts.

In practice, international water disputes have moved away from the extreme positions implied by these two doctrines and toward a doctrine of *equitable and reasonable use*. Although this narrows the likely range of disagreement, it does not provide clear property rights. In the absence of enforceable property rights, the strongest, most clever, and most advantageously positioned countries can claim and use the resource with little concern for the impact on others. Opportunities for coordinated management may be lost in the acrimony over rights to the resource and obligations to mitigate any adverse effects imposed on others. When the interdependence among countries is unidirectional, such as with the impacts of an upstream user on the quantity and quality of water downstream, the upstream country may have little incentive to limit its use of the river other than the threat of retaliation by the downstream user. But even when the interdependence is mutual and all countries could benefit from a cooperative development and allocation of a basin's water resources, the incentive to arrive at an efficient and mutually agreeable strategy may not exist.

The institutions controlling water use are often rooted in an era when the resource was not considered to be scarce and transfers were viewed as unnecessary or unimportant. Cultural and religious considerations that view water as too important or too sacred to have its use determined by the impersonal outcome of markets may inhibit the evolution of institutions that view water as a scarce resource that must be allocated among competing uses. Equity considerations and historical use have been more important than efficiency in the management of both domestic and internationally shared water resources. There are relatively few precedents that demonstrate the potential advantages of efficient integrated management of an entire hydrologic unit. Yet, as water becomes increasingly scarce, the potential benefits of integrated management and of institutions that enable scarce resources to be transferred among competing uses in response to changing conditions will grow. Institutions that perpetuate inefficient water use will become increasingly costly and unstable. Inflexible and inefficient international agreements, which must be self-enforcing, may not be sustainable.

3. CONCLUSION

Based on the above analysis of the demographic, pollution, and resource situation likely to prevail in twenty years, we can examine what tasks will arise for the U.S. military in 2015 arising out of environmental stresses. We start with the least likely and proceed to the most probable.

GENERAL CHAOS

Since the end of the Cold War, armed conflict seems to be less a clash of states or political movements and more a struggle among ethnic groups over control of land in resource-poor areas. If the prototypical 1980s conflicts were the Iran-Iraq war and the Afghanistan or Nicaraguan civil wars, the stereotypical mid-1990s conflicts seem to be the slaughter in Rwanda, the battles between tiny ethnic groups in the Caucasus region, or the ethnic cleansing in the former Yugoslavia. Warfare there seems premodern: a clash of peoples rather than armies, with no organized structure to the fighting forces, no clear separation between civilians and soldiers, and no political decisionmakers able to dictate strategy and negotiate a peace.

This may indeed be the trend of warfare, but it is by no means clear that this has anything to do with population, pollution, and resource problems. Rolling all these developments into one ball can make for dramatic reading, as in Robert Kaplan's widely noted article about "the coming anarchy." [14] Kaplan seems to suggest that the community of sovereign states could dissolve into chaos, as governments are unable to respond effectively to a global resource crunch, to ever more powerful transnational forces (benign and malign), and to fragmentation of the state into local communities and ethnic groups. Overwhelmed by burgeoning populations and declining resources, the state will become unable to contain social conflicts that boil up as crime gangs and ethnic cleansers. Some have therefore suggested, that our overriding national security task should be "preventing the causes of global chaos." [15]

The dissolution of the world into anarchy does not seem to be a plausible development by 2015. It is difficult to see how the community of prosperous and democratic nations could be overwhelmed within the next 20 years, given that there are few indications in 1995 that any such resource shortage is affecting the advanced industrial states. Whether chaos could overwhelm the world order after 2015 is beyond the scope of this report, but it is worth noting that the general trend identified here is for human social problems, from global warming to the population explosion, to evoke corrective responses, both through government action and through changes in private behavior.

An appealing part of the chaos story is that the world is facing escalating pollution and resource-depletion problems. That may be the case. However, that does not imply that the U.S. military will have an important role in responding to such problems. The potential for peaceful conflict resolution was discussed above. In the event that negotiations lead to an impasse, the U.S. military is still unlikely to get involved in responding to global pollution issues. In order to secure compliance from noncooperating countries, the most likely route is to use a variety of economic sanctions and rewards, e.g., trade restrictions and privileges. In other cases, the majority of countries may simply feel that it is not worth the effort to gain cooperation and will simply absorb the additional costs among themselves. Military force is not likely to be useful in most cases because of the diffuse source of the problem and the probable judgment that any loss of life would not be worth the benefit gained. There are some causes where the use of force to redress a problem might be deemed technically feasible:—for instance, if the pollution were caused by a small number of highly defined sources (say, Indian CFC production facilities) and if the offending sites were located in a small number of countries (say, China as the source of nearly all the foreign-caused acid rain failing on Japan). Overall, however, the political prospect that the U.S. Armed Forces would be assigned any such mission seems highly unlikely.

FAILED STATES

While general chaos is unlikely in 2015, it is quite probable that there will be a number of countries in which the state has failed--the government is unable or unwilling to guarantee the safety of the populace from disasters, natural, human (e.g., ethnic slaughter), or a mixture of the two (e.g., famine).

It seems intuitively obvious to connect state failure with environmental stress. The classic theory of state collapse generated by population and resource pressures is that of Homer-Dixon, Boutwell, and Rathjens.[16] Their framework is helpful because of its simplicity, clarity and flexibility. They argue that population growth and unequal access to resources lead to increased scarcity of resources like cropland and water. Scarcity of resources decreases economic productivity and increases migration to cities. The growing urban population and the agricultural productivity decline reduce the state's revenue and increase its spending as it deals with the deteriorating circumstances. The result is to weaken the financial and political stability of the state. The combination of problems weakens the state, which eventually leads to ethnic conflict and social disorder

What is missing from the Homer-Dixon et al. framework is the role of governance, social values, and ethnic or religious tensions. These are variables that interact with economic and resource-availability factors in ways that are hard to estimate or predict. However, they seem to be on the forefront of the reasons that most state failures to date have occurred. It is instructive to observe the collapse of the state in mid-income countries with failed governments like Yugoslavia or Lebanon, both richer and better endowed with resources than some of their stable neighbors. Contrast this to the experience of some of the world's most resource-short and overpopulated countries, like Bangladesh and Malawi, that have had better governance. Democracy lets India—a country racked by poverty, vicious ethnic and religious splits, and rapidly-growing population in a densely-packed land—contain its conflicts.

The Homer-Dixon et al. model plays down plays what may be the most stressful environmental factor in the next 20 years: the challenge of creating productive employment for the growing number of young adults. With the labor force in developing countries growing by 30 million each year, there is a real potential for mass youth unemployment that could feed radical populist movements. The unrest in Algeria may be a harbinger of the problems that will arise in countries that do not successfully meet the job-creation challenge.

Based on current trends of which states have serious problems with governance, social values, ethnic/religious tension, and environmental stress, it seems likely that most of the failed states in 2015 will be in Africa, South Asia, and the greater Middle East (including its northern edges on the fringes of the ex-Communist world: the Balkans, the Caucasus, and Central Asia). On the whole, these are not areas close to the United States in any important strategic sense: geographically, historically, economically, or politically. It is therefore not obvious what vital strategic U.S. interests will be threatened by most developing-world state failures. There could of course be some failed states near to the United States or in areas of historic and strategic U.S. interest—e.g., the Caribbean basin or those parts of the Middle East of most interest to the United States (the Persian Gulf and Israel and its neighbors).

Even though most failed states will not threaten U.S. strategic interests, they may challenge important U.S. values, such as democracy and human rights. The United States may be drawn to intervene militarily in some such cases because the offense to our values and because of the scale of the suffering. However, it does not seem likely that, in this time of reduced resources and increased concern about problems at home, the United States will make a commitment to intervene in every such case. The United States may well encourage other major powers to act in those countries that are more important historically and strategically to them than to the United States If the United States faces other demands on its military power that are immediately related to national strategic interests, those are likely to take priority over intervention in a failed state. In short, U.S. intervention in failed states is likely to be selective, not automatic.

Failed states may well produce refugee exoduses. The risk of such mass migrations will be an important factor in the decision to intervene in a failed state. The U.S. military is most likely to be engaged in circumstances that threaten to produce large migrant flows to the United States However, sudden mass migrations not involving the United States may still concern U.S. strategic interests if they threaten to convert the internal problems of one failed state into a crisis involving several states.

TENSIONS AMONG STATES

Environmental stresses could involve the U.S. military by making tensions among sovereign states more likely and more intense. In most cases, these tensions will be resolved well short of armed conflict. Peaceful conflict resolution mechanisms seem more likely to be employed (with varying degrees of success), in part because it is not obvious how military force would be useful in resolving many demographic, pollution, or resource problems. In environmental disputes, the pressure applied by one state against another is much more likely to be economic than military.

However, some environmental stresses may contribute to armed conflict among states. Transborder resource conflicts could well have this effect for three reasons:

❑   Peaceful conflict-resolution mechanisms are inadequate

❑   The conflicts stir strong emotions

❑   Military force can be applied for a clear and specific purpose, i.e., gaining control over the disputed resource.

Perhaps the shortage of some resource, such as oil, will tempt one nation to grab part of the territory of another, though the poor success rate of such ventures would surely give pause to any rogue state contemplating aggression.

While environmental stress may be a contributor to interstate conflict, it is not likely to be the fundamental cause. A transborder conflict is unlikely to escalate into warfare unless the states in question have generally bad relations, for otherwise they are likely to work out some kind of *modus vivendi*. A resource grab occurs only in the case of an aggressive government, which has much more to do with political failure than with any environmental factor.

Three areas in which there could well be transborder resource disputes are regions of intense concern to the United States. First is the Persian Gulf, where the great riches of the oil reserves raises the temperature in the tensions between Persian and Arab civilizations and in the dynastic border disputes involving each of the states in the Arabian Peninsula. Second is the Arab-Israeli theater, where water supplies are scarce and political ill-will abundant. Third is the South China Sea, which may contain large oil deposits (as suggested by the $30 billion project in nearby Indonesia waters, which will be in full production by 2015) and where nationalist fervor is matched only by the importance of the region as a transit zone for commercial shipping.

While the prospects are low for open warfare in 2015 over transborder resources, the stakes in these three areas at the least will be sufficiently high that the U.S. military could well be tasked to maintain a presence in order to contribute to regional stability and to be ready to project power on a large scale if needed to come to the aid of regional states challenged by an aggressor.

NOTES

1. World Bank, *World Population Projections 1994-95*, and United Nations Fund for Population Activities, *The State of the World's Population 1994*.

2. Bryant Robey, Shea O. Rutstein, and Leo Morris, "The Fertility Decline in Developing Countries," *Scientific American* (December 1993), 601. In a similar vein, see John Bongaarts, "Population Policy Options in the Developing World," *Science* (February 11, 1994), 771-776.

3. This, and the next two points, are drawn from Gil Loescher, *Refugee Movements and International Security*, Adelphi Paper 268, International Institute for Strategic Studies, London (Summer 1992).

4. Doris M. Meissner, Robert D. Hormats, Antonio Garrigues Walker, Shijuro Ogata, *International Migration Challenges in a New Era* (New York: The Trilateral Commission, 1993), 89.

5. Andrew Natsios, President George Bush's special coordinator of Somali relief and a Lieutenant Colonel in a U.S. Army Reserve civil affairs unit, "Food Through Force: Humanitarian Intervention and U.S. Policy," *The Washington Quarterly* (Winter 1994), 140.

6. For an example of grave concern, see Richard Bissell, "The Natural Resource Wars: Let Them Eat Trees," *The Washington Quarterly* (Winter 1994), 149-165.

7. Hans Landsberg, *Natural Resources for U.S. Growth* (Baltimore, Maryland: Johns Hopkins University Press, 1964), 250.

8. Bob Tippee, "Questions Cloud Outlook for Oil Production Capacity Growth in the Middle East," *Oil and Gas Journal* (July 11, 1994), 33-36.

9. Hans Landsberg, *Natural Resources for U.S. Growth*, 183.

10. Kenneth Frederick and Roger Sedjo, *America's Renewable Resources* (Washington, D.C.: Resources for the Future, 1991), 19.

11. Kenneth Frederick and Roger Sedjo, *America's Renewable Resources*, 19.

12. Hans Landsberg, *Natural Resources for U.S. Growth*, 248.

13. There is a vast literature on water conflicts in the Middle East. A good summary statement is Peter Gleick, "Water, War and Peace in the Middle East," *Environment* (April 1994), 6-15 and 35-42. On South Asia, see Shaukat Hussain, *Environmental Issues and Security in South Asia*, Adelphi Paper 262, International Institute for Strategic Studies (Winter 1991).

14. Robert Kaplan, "The Coming Anarchy," *Atlantic* (February 1994), 44-76.

15. Jeremy Rosner, "Is Chaos America's Real Enemy?", *Washington Post* (August 14, 1994), C1-C2, discusses the appeal that this thesis (and Kaplan's article) have to top policy makers in the Clinton administration. See also Daniel Moynihan, *Pandemonium*.

16. Thomas Homer-Dixon, Jeffrey Boutwell, and George Rathjens, "Environmental Scarcity and Violent Conflict," *Scientific American* (February 1993)). For a guide to the literature on this topic, see Thomas Homer-Dixon, "Population Growth and Conflict," *Environmental Dimensions of Security*. For empirical examples, see Thomas HomerDixon, "Environmental Scarcities and Violent Conflict: Evidence from Cases," *International Security* (Summer 1994).

III. COALITIONS

Stephen M. Walt is Professor of Political Science at the University of Chicago. He has been a Resident Associate at the Carnegie Endowment for International Peace and a Guest Scholar at the Brookings Institution and has received fellowships from the MacArthur Foundation and the U.S. Institute for Peace. Dr. Walt is the author of *The Origins of Alliances* (Cornell 1987), which received the 1988 Edgar S. Furnis National Security Book Award, and *Revolution and War* (Cornell 1996). Dr. Walt received his B.A. From Stanford University and his master's and doctoral degrees from the University of California at Berkeley.

1. THE NECESSITY OF COALITIONS

Part III provides a framework for thinking about the future formation and management of U.S. military coalitions and alliances. History has shown that the formation, management, and performance of military coalitions can have powerful effects on both the security of individual states and the stability of the international system. Over the centuries, city-states, empires, feudal fiefs, and modern nation-states have joined forces to increase their power and enhance their security. In fact, such arrangements appear to ubiquitous in the relations between political units. The ability to form effective military coalitions is a formidable asset for any great power, which means that prudent strategic planning requires careful consideration of the forces that are likely to bring states together or drive them apart.

The United States is no exception to this basic strategic principle. Despite its isolationist traditions, the United States has relied upon allied support on numerous occasions in the past, especially since its rise to great-power status at the end of the 19th century. The United States was a key member of the victorious coalitions in both world wars and subsequently led the coalition that fought the Korean War under the auspices of the United Nations. Support from allies in Europe and Japan was a major U.S. asset throughout the Cold War (especially when compared with the Soviet alliance system), and the United States has also profited from its ties to states such as Israel, Australia, New Zealand, Saudi Arabia, and others.[1] The value of allied support was reaffirmed during the 1991 Gulf War; although the United States provided the bulk of the military power, support from other states either facilitated military action or enhanced the legitimacy of U.S. intervention, or both.

The end of the Cold War has reopened the issues of U.S. alliance management and its preparations for coalition warfare. During the Cold War, the clarity of the Soviet threat and the basic stability of international political structures held the main coalitions constant for nearly four decades, and realignments were usually due to internal factors (such as a radical regime change) rather than external events.[2] The collapse of the Soviet Union has drastically reduced, if not vitiated, the original rationale behind many existing alliances and coalitions (e.g., NATO); iover the next two decades, the United States is likely to face a diverse array of lesser threats instead of a single, overriding adversary. The Gulf War, the ill-fated intervention in Somalia, peace operations in the Balkans, Rwanda, and Haiti, and the ongoing diplomatic alignment with regard to North Korea's nuclear program suggest that major international issues will have to be dealt with in the context of some kind of coalition. Indeed, because sustained military interventions by democracies must have broad public support, political leaders are quick to orchestrate multinational responses to crises around the globe. As such, coalition operations are becoming a standard operating procedure, and there is little evidence that even strong-minded political leaders will be able to buck this trend in the next 20 years (see chart). Moreover, although the United States will remain the only power capable of major military action on a global scale for some time to come, the relative decline of U.S. military power is already making it more difficult for the United States to act unilaterally. Thus, the assumption of this report is the following: *if the United States wishes to maintain an active overseas presence into the 21st century, its foreign policy and military strategy will have to be tailored to coalition warfare.* Indeed, unilateral action could further undermine existing alliances and even precipitate the formation of anti-U.S. coalitions. Conversely, an excessive American retrenchment from its postwar alliance leadership role could render such alliances and coalitions "paper tigers" incapable of meaningful military action. Another alternative, at least for conflicts in which no vital U.S. interests were at stake, could entail a sharper division of labor between the U.S. and its coalition partners. That division of labor is captured by the term "vertical coalition," marked by an asymmetrical burden-sharing arrangement in which the U.S. provides information and information-based systems and America's coalition partners supply the troops and weapons systems. Part III focuses on four issues.

❑ Why do states join coalitions? What are the different *theories* that explain a decision to join a coalition? What do they imply for U.S. efforts to form and/or lead them in the future?

❑ What are the main *obstacles* to forming an effective coalition? Even when several states have a clear incentive to join forces, why do some coalitions succeed and others fail?

❑ What are the different *structural characteristics* of different coalitions, and how do these features affect their performance?

❑ How are these issues likely to evolve over the next two decades? Even if perfect prediction is impossible, what are the areas of certainty and uncertainty that will shape the formation and performance of future coalitions, and what lessons should U.S. strategic planners draw from these considerations?

To clarify basic terminology, a *military coalition* is used here to denote a formal or informal arrangement for joint military action by two or more states. This definition assumes a tangible commitment to mutual (though not necessarily identical) support and assumes that severing the relationship or failing to honor it would be costly. This definition includes both formal alliances (where the nature of the commitment and each member's contributions are precisely demarcated in a formal treaty) and informal or *ad hoc* agreements for security cooperation that arise in response to some immediate contingency. Including both formal and informal arrangements makes sense because states may be willing to provide extensive support to one another even in the absence of a

Recent Coalitions :

Since the end of the Cold War, the United States has found coalition partners from all over the globe. Some of the more significant recent coalitions were:

❏ *Desert Shield/Storm:* In 1990, the United States deployed 500,000 troops to the Persian Gulf as part of a U.S.-led coalition force to defend Saudi Arabia. In January 1991, the U.S.-led coalition commenced a 6week military campaign that liberated Kuwait and crushed the Iraqi armed forces. Coalition forces, particularly from key NATO allies, such as Britain and France, played an important military role in the victory.

❏ *Southern Watch:* Since 1992, U.S. and coalition aircraft have enforced a no-fly zone over southern Iraq.

❏ *Provide Comfort:* Under way since the end of the Gulf War, this operation maintains a secure environment that permits humanitarian assistance to flow to the endangered Kurdish population of northern Iraq. Multinational operations include approximately 1,500 U.S. military personnel and some 50 aircraft sorties per day, on average, from NATO bases in Turkey.

❏ *Vigilant Warrior:* In October 1994, after two Iraqi Republican Guard divisions massed on the Kuwaiti border, the United States deployed a Marine Expeditionary Unit, elements of a heavy Army division, a carrier task force, and additional land-based aircraft to reinforce security partners Kuwait and Saudi Arabia.

❏ *Uphold Democracy:* In September 1994, the United States entered Haiti peacefully to oversee the return of the country's popularly elected government (ending President Jean-Bertrand Aristide's 3-year exile) and the departure of the nation's military leaders. The use of U.S. military power in an effort to restore a democratically elected government was the first such operation in the Western Hemisphere ever authorized by the United Nations. Various regional nations pledged support to help provide civil control after the U.S. military operation reined in the armed forces, police, and paramilitary groups.

❏ *Deny Flight:* Beginning in April 1993, about 1,700 U.S. military personnel stationed in Europe participated with NATO allies to enforce a ban on military flights over Bosnia, monitoring the U.N. protection areas and providing close air support to U.N. peacekeepers in Bosnia when called upon.

❏ *Able Sentry:* Since the spring of 1993, about 500 U.S. troops have participated in the U.N. observer force, now called the U.N. Preventive Deployment in the former Yugoslav republic of Macedonia, providing a stabilizing presence and preventing the conflict in other regions of the former Yugoslavia from spilling over into Macedonia.

❏ *Sharp Guard:* Starting in April 1993, three U.S. naval vessels and approximately 7,800 U.S. personnel participated regularly with NATO allies in maritime enforcement of sanctions against Serbia in the Adriatic Sea, with intermittent support from other assets of the U.S. Sixth Fleet. As with *Deny Flight,* Sharp Guard was terminated in December 1995 with the establishment of IFOR.

❏ *Support Hope:* From June through September 1994, some 2,000 U.S. military personnel from Europe deployed to Africa to organize and carry out emergency humanitarian relief operations for refugees fleeing a brutal civil war in Rwanda. While the U.S. operation was unilateral, it directly supported multinational governmental and nongovernmental efforts at providing humanitarian support. Moreover, as the U.S. pulled out in the autumn of 1994, its major Asian ally, Japan, dispatched peacekeeping forces to support refugee camps in Zaire.

❏ *Provide Relief:* From August 1992 until March 1993, the U.S. conducted a military airlift from Mombasa, Kenya, to deliver goods to Somali refugees. The U.S. also led the Unified Interim Task Force from December 1992 to May 1993, which was a large-scale coalition effort to stem mass starvation.

formal treaty, and because the presence of a formal agreement often says relatively little about the actual degree of commitment.[3]

This definition focuses on agreements to cooperate in the use of military force, including United Nations Chapter VI and Chapter VII peace operations. However, it *excludes* cooperation that is purely economic or commercial in nature; states with extensive economic links are not necessarily part of a coalition. It also excludes cooperation for purely humanitarian purposes (such as disaster relief) as well as cooperation in purely diplomatic activities (such as voting behavior in the United Nations General Assembly or negotiating positions in other international forums), *unless* such arrangements are accompanied by a decision to collaborate in the use of military force.

2. THEORIES OF COALITION FORMATION

Why do states join coalitions, and what determines the partners they will prefer? As stated in Chapter One, alliances and coalitions are the means by which states pursue common or at least complementary interests. In other words, the primary purpose behind most coalitions is to combine the members' capabilities in ways that promote their respective interests. Coalitions can take many forms (e.g., offensive or defensive, symmetrical or asymmetrical, formal or informal), but the common thread in virtually all such arrangements is each member's desire to improve its relative position by collaborating with at least one other state.[4]

BALANCING BEHAVIOR

Despite the end of the Cold War, or perhaps increasingly because of it, the U.S. and other states will form coalitions over the next two decades for much the same fundamental reasons they have in previous decades. The most fundamental reason to form a coalition is to oppose an external threat. In particular, states form coalitions in order to balance against the most threatening state (or coalition) that they face. The rationale for this tendency is straightforward: because no supreme authority exists to protect states from each other, states facing a possible threat will join forces with others in order to amass sufficient power to deter or defeat an attack. Nor is such a supreme authority likely to be created in the span of the next 20 years.

The foregoing explanation is usually framed in terms of *power*; states with lesser capabilities are presumed to combine against stronger powers in order to prevent them from dominating.[5] As Stephen Walt has shown, this view is useful but incomplete, because it neglects several other factors that leaders will consider when making alliance decisions. For example, a state may prefer to ally with the *stronger* of two powers if the weaker side is more dangerous for other reasons. Thus, it is more accurate to say that states form coalitions to balance against *threats*, and power is only one element in their calculations. In general, the level of threat that states face will be a function of four distinct factors: aggregate power, geographic proximity, offensive capabilities, and aggressive intentions.

Aggregate Power

Other things being equal, the greater a state's total resources (e.g., population, industrial capacity, military strength, etc.), the greater harm it can inflict on others. Thus, the greater a state's *aggregate power*, the larger the potential threat. Recognizing this, the traditional aim of U.S. grand strategy has been to prevent any single power from controlling the combined resources of Eurasia, because such an agglomeration of power could pose a serious threat to U.S. security. England's traditional reliance on a balance of power policy reflected the same motivations, and contemporary concerns over China's economic and military growth betray a similar sensitivity. A state's aggregate power is not the sole determinant of threat, of course, but it is always an important one.

Geographic Proximity

Because the ability to project power declines with distance, states that are nearby are usually more dangerous than those that are far away.[6] As a result, states are more likely to form coalitions in response to threats from their neighbors, and they will prefer allies that are geographically separate. Students of diplomatic history have long been taught that "neighbors of neighbors are friends," and the tendency for coalition networks to resemble checkerboards was observed by the Indian political philosopher Kautilya in the fourth century.[7] During the Cold War, this factor helps explain why regional powers usually preferred to rely on support from a distant superpower rather than on cooperation with other regional actors. The reason was obvious: the superpower could do more to help, and allying with a neighbor can be dangerous if that neighbor becomes too strong as a result. This motive also explains why the superpowers' efforts to recruit regional clients were only partly successful. Although Moscow and Washington sought allies primarily to counter each other, their clients in the developing world were usually more worried about regional or internal threats and relatively unconcerned about the global balance of power.[8]

Offensive Capabilities

States with large offensive capabilities—defined as the ability to threaten the sovereignty or territorial integrity of other states—pose a greater threat than states whose capabilities are designed primarily to defend their own territory. As a state's offensive capabilities increase, therefore (either because its military expenditures are growing or because its armed forces are being tailored for offensive warfare), other states will be more inclined to form a coalition against it. The ability to undermine other regimes via propaganda or subversion can be a potent source of threat as well, which explains why revolutionary states espousing universalist ideologies are usually regarded as dangerous even when they are militarily weak.[9]

Offensive Intentions

States with aggressive aims are obviously more dangerous than states that are satisfied with the status quo. A weak state with bellicose ambitions, such as Libya or Iran, is likely to find itself isolated as other states join together to contain the danger. Other things being equal, therefore, the belief that a state harbors offensive intentions will increase the likelihood that a countervailing coalition will form against it.

Taken together, these factors explain why potential hegemons like Napoleonic France, Wilhelmine Germany and Nazi Germany eventually faced an overwhelming opposing coalition: each of these states were great powers lying in close proximity to others and each combined large offensive capabilities with extremely bellicose aims. The same factors explain why the Soviet Union was overmatched during the Cold War: it was the second most powerful state in the system, it lay in close proximity to the medium powers of Europe and Asia, it possessed a large military establishment whose forces and doctrine were tailored for offensive wars of conquest, and it never publicly abandoned its commitment to world revolution. Although the United States had greater overall capabilities, its distance from the other centers of world power made it the perfect ally for the medium powers that were most directly threatened by the Soviet Union.

"Balance-of-threat" theory also explains why the United States was able to assemble such a large and cohesive coalition during the Gulf War. Although Iraq was not a great power, its military forces were growing, its conquest of Kuwait threatened Western oil supplies, and Saddam Hussein's foreign and domestic conduct suggested that he had extremely aggressive ambitions and was willing to run impressive risks to achieve them. Adroit diplomacy helped bring the coalition into existence, and to sustain it in spite of myriad asymmetries among the coalition partners, but the essential pre-conditions for an effective coalition were clearly present as well.[10]

BANDWAGONING BEHAVIOR

Although the desire to balance threats is the main reason why coalitions form, some states may prefer to "jump on the bandwagon" and join forces with the dominant (or most threatening) power rather than attempting to form a coalition against it. This may be done either for defensive or offensive reasons: some states may seek the stronger side in order to appease it while others join the strong side in order to profit from its victory.

Several factors will affect a state's propensity to bandwagon. First, weak states are more inclined to bandwagon than strong states, because they can do little to affect the outcome and must choose the winning side at all costs.[11] The likelihood of bandwagoning also increases when a state faces an imminent threat and potential coalition partners are unavailable. Even if such a state *prefers* to balance, it may be forced to bandwagon if it cannot obtain adequate allied support. Third, bandwagoning is more likely to occur in the latter stages of a war, when the outcome is clear and states rush in either to curry favor with the victor(s) or to extract spoils from the vanquished. Lastly, highly revisionist states will be more inclined to bandwagon, because they are especially interested in reaping the benefits from victory and must take pains to pick the likely winners.[12] Benito Mussolini's declaration of war against France in 1940 offers an example of all three factors; Italy was a comparatively weak state yet had highly revisionist aims, and Mussolini waited until France's defeat was apparent before declaring war.

Although statesmen commonly fear that potential partners will align with the strongest or most threatening power (i.e., many statesmen seem to believe that bandwagoning is extremely common), this fear receives relatively little historical support. Since the Thirty Years' War, every attempt to achieve hegemony in Europe has been thwarted by a powerful balancing coalition, and similar examples from recent history include the Gulf War coalition, the Association of Southeast Asian Nations (ASEAN), the Sino-American *rapprochement* in the 1970s, the formation of the Gulf Cooperation Council and the U.S. tilt against Iran during the Iran-Iraq war, and the coalition of Front-Line States against

South Africa during the 1970s and 1980s.[13] Although such a hypothesis may seem overly mechanistic for a description of interstate behavior, this tendency should not surprise us; balancing should be preferred for the simple reason that no national leader can be completely sure what others will do. Bandwagoning is dangerous because it increases the capabilities available to a threatening power and requires placing trust in its continued benevolence.[14] Because perceptions of intent are often unreliable and intentions can change overnight, it is usually safer to balance against potential threats rather than taking their continued forbearance on faith.

OTHER MOTIVES FOR COALITION FORMATION

Although the desire to balance threats is the main reason why states join coalitions, several other motives can play a role as well. Some coalitions are inspired by *ideological solidarity*, where states with similar domestic orders join forces for largely idealistic reasons. Indeed, democracies may well fight other democracies on occasion, but it seems axiomatic that democracies tend to ally with other democracies far easier than with authoritarian states. This ideological solidarity motive helps explain U.S. efforts to support fledgling democracies and earlier Soviet support for "progressive forces" in the developing world, as well as Iran's willingness to back Islamic fundamentalists in Sudan, Lebanon and elsewhere. Ideological solidarity is usually a relatively weak glue; most states will abandon this criterion when serious external threats arise. Moreover, a common ideology can also be a potent source of contention, as the Sino-Soviet split and the sorry history of the pan-Arab movement both suggest.[15] An important partial exception to this generalization may well pertain to America's inner-circle alliances. Leaving aside the normative question as to whether U.S. policy should be determined in such a manner, it seems self-evident that, to a degree far greater than most European or Asian major powers, the United States makes alliance policy on the basis of both values and interests. There are many reasons for this, the chief one perhaps being that the perpetuation of liberal Western values is viewed as virtually inseparable from vital U.S. interests.

Another reason to form a coalition is to enhance one's influence over the other members. By offering support or protection to a weaker state, great powers can manipulate their conduct in order to advance their own interests.[16] This motive is closely related to balancing behavior; the weaker side in effect gives up some of its autonomy in exchange for its patron's protection, while patrons use security guarantees, economic and military aid and other forms of persuasion if not bribery to cement the relationship and enhance their own influence. These mechanisms rarely create a coalition by themselves, however, and care will be needed to prevent efforts to manipulate one's clients from generating a hostile backlash.[17]

A third reason to form a coalition is to dampen conflict within the international system as a whole. This type of coalition can take the form of a large-scale collective security system (like the League of Nations) or a more limited great-power concert (like the Concert of Europe after the Napoleonic Wars). Instead of forming a coalition against a particular threat, such arrangements seek to prevent war by threatening a collective "all for one" response to any overt act of aggression, even if one of the members of the coalition is responsible. Concert systems also seek to check suspicions by providing a mechanism for peaceful consultation and negotiation, thereby dampening the "security dilemma" and facilitating the peaceful resolution of disputes.

Although history suggests that both collective-security and concert approaches should be viewed with great skepticism, they remain a popular prescription for the post-Cold War security environment (especially in Europe). Indeed, the rhetoric of "collective security" is still invoked to justify actions, such as Operation *Desert Storm,* that were actually taken largely for self-interested reasons.[18]

IMPLICATIONS

Two important implications may be drawn from the analysis thus far. First, the ability of the United States to forge and manage future coalitions will be largely a function of the external security environment. States do not join coalitions and fight wars for altruistic or sentimental reasons; rather, vital decisions such as these ordinarily reflect careful considerations of self-interest. Although shared values and similar political systems can facilitate negotiation for an alliance and smooth potential rifts within the resulting coalition (suggesting that shared interests and shared values make for the strongest alliances), we should not expect other states to join us unless they believe it is in their interest to do so. This means that if other states do not see themselves as threatened, the United States will not be able to entice (or coerce) them into a coalition. Of course, if the external environment is benign, we will have less need to. However, in a reversal of the Cold War era, the post-Cold War era seems more likely to see states attempting to ally with the U.S. when, from an American perspective, there may be scant reason to do so. The current debate over whether to expand NATO—e.g., to incorporate the Visegrad states of Poland, Hungary, the Czech Republic and Slovakia—is a case in point. These states undoubtedly would like a NATO security umbrella and they may indeed be threatened one day; but the near-term threat to their security is far from apparent, a fact suggested by the diminished defense budgets of these Central European states.

Second, the U.S. ability to form and lead future coalitions will depend on its own capacity to contribute to these arrangements. Although states *prefer* to balance against threats, they will find this option less appealing if they do not believe it will succeed. Thus, even if the United States gradually relies less on formal alliances such as NATO and more on flexible and *ad hoc* coalitions, it will still have to possess the military assets that have made it an attractive partner in the past. Nothing could be more quixotic than for the United States to reduce its leading-edge warfighting and power-projection capabilities— including the essential forward-based posture that makes our unique global reach possible, while pursuing an ephemeral objective of multinationalism for its own sake. In short, coalition support should be seen as an adjunct to U.S. military power, not a substitute.

It does not follow, however, that the United States must or should contribute in the same ways to future coalition partners that it has to previous coalition partners. As power-projection becomes increasingly costly and/or dangerous for the United States, and where American interests are deemed less than vital, it will be increasingly attractive for the United States to resort to what might be called "vertical coalitions." Because future conflicts may be heavily dependent upon information and information systems, in some situations in which the U.S. Armed Forces are called upon to assist coalition partners it may be in the U.S. interest to limit its contribution to information-intensive support. In contrast, coalition partners generally may be expected to provide the bulk of soldiers and weaponry. The concept of vertical coalitions is elaborated upon in Part IV, which examines the future impact of information-based warfare on the U.S. Armed Forces.

3. MANAGING FUTURE COALITIONS

When states form coalitions swiftly and efficiently (in other words, when the balancing process works smoothly), and when this tendency is widely understood, aggression is discouraged because even highly ambitious leaders will anticipate opposition to any aggressive moves. For example, if Saddam Hussein had known that the seizure of Kuwait would generate a vast coalition of powers seeking to expel his forces and weaken his regime, it is unlikely that he would have acted as he did. Similarly, if Saddam Hussein's troop movements in October 1994 were intended as a prelude to another invasion of Kuwait—as opposed to a feint designed to bolster his domestic support—then the Iraqi dictator mistakenly believed that the United States and United Nations were overly distracted with other global problems. President Clinton's swift military response left Saddam Hussein with no doubt as to the consequences of further aggression. Likewise, the rapid establishment of the Western alliance in 1949-1950 made it clear to the Soviet Union that any overt act of aggression would be met by a combined Western response, thereby enhancing the security of the West and helping preserve peace between East and West for more than 40 years.

Aggressors will be harder to deter when balancing takes place slowly or inefficiently, and the probability of war will perforce increase. For instance, although the Western states did balance against the growing threat from Nazi Germany, their efforts to do so were not particularly rapid or efficient. Not only were Britain and France distracted and diverted by threats in several separate theaters (making it harder to focus all their attention on Germany), but Adolf Hitler was a master of dissimulation who carefully cloaked the scope of his ambitions. As a result, his future opponents did not recognize the true magnitude of the threat until very late. Efforts to form a countervailing coalition were also impaired by ideological antipathies among Britain, France, and the Soviet Union, by rivalries among Germany's Eastern European neighbors, and by the East European states' refusal to ally with Joseph Stalin (whose embrace they correctly judged to be every bit as threatening as Hitler's). For these and other reasons, the effort to balance against Germany fell short of the level necessary for successful deterrence, especially given Hitler's extraordinary desire for war.[19]

The efficiency of the balancing process will also play an important role in determining success in wartime. The ability to coordinate strategy and maintain adequate levels of effort will maximize the likelihood of victory; by contrast, disputes over wartime priorities and extensive efforts to pass the costs of the war onto one's allies) will impair any coalition's efforts and may lead to an unnecessary defeat. In the wars of the French Revolution, for example, the First and Second Coalitions against France were undermined and ultimately defeated in large part because they could not coordinate their military activities and because the member states focused on maximizing their individual gains while trying to shove the burden of defeating France onto each other. By contrast, although the victorious coalitions in World Wars I and II experienced repeated disputes over strategy and relative levels of effort, these disagreements did not undermine their battlefield performance significantly.[20]

These examples reveal that one cannot assume that balancing coalitions will always form, or will always operate well enough to succeed. And this point raises the obvious question: what are the main obstacles to effective and efficient coalition formation?

CONFLICTING INTERESTS

States are unlikely to form a coalition if their interests are opposed. Forming an effective coalition will be impossible if one state regards another as especially dangerous but other states do not share its perceptions of threat. Thus, French officials at the Paris Peace Conference in 1919 repeatedly advocated joint Western intervention to reverse the Bolshevik Revolution but were unable to persuade British and U.S. leaders that such a step was necessary or advisable.[21] Alternatively, other states may recognize that a particular power is dangerous but conclude that their own interests are not involved. Thus, U.S. efforts to isolate Iran after the seizure of U.S. hostages in 1980 were undermined by the fact that key American allies did not see this act as a threat to their own interests. Lastly, states may be ineligible for a coalition because they prefer the other side. During the Cold War, for example, the United States and Soviet Union interpreted most international events in a zero-sum fashion (if it was good for one side, it was bad for the other). Because their interests were in conflict on most issues, they rarely if ever saw each other as prospective coalition partners.[22] In general, the greater the divergence in state interests, the more difficult it will be to form a coalition among them.

COMPETING PRESCRIPTIONS

Even when states agree that a particular power is dangerous and share an interest in reducing the danger, they may disagree over how to respond. If a particular state appears to have aggressive aims, for instance, some states may favor a strategy of accommodation while others advocate efforts to contain or overthrow it. During the 1980s, for example, the United States and the members of the so-called Contadora Group (Mexico, Venezuela, Colombia and Panama) generally agreed that the Sandinista regime in Nicaragua posed a threat to regional stability. They disagreed completely, however, on both the magnitude of the threat and the best way to deal with it. Believing that the Sandinistas could be accommodated, contained, and deradicalized, the Central American states opposed military intervention in favor of negotiations for a regional security pact. The United States was convinced that the Sandinistas were irredeemably pro-Soviet and utterly untrustworthy, however, and actively sought to overthrow them. Thus, although the United States and the Contadora group had similar interests and goals (both wanted to preserve the stability of the hemisphere), competing prescriptions for how to achieve these objectives impaired their ability to form a unified coalition.

Similar dynamics can be found in the protracted effort to formulate a unified policy towards North Korea's nuclear weapons program. The major powers of China, Russia, Japan, South Korea and the United States generally agree on the desirability of maintaining regional stability and, only slightly less so, on curbing nuclear proliferation in Northeast Asia. However, the major regional powers faced repeated difficulties in agreeing over the means of bringing North Korea into compliance with international safeguards. The October 21, 1994 nuclear framework accord negotiated by the United States and North Korea reflected a lowest common-denominator consensus among those powers, a fact that led to sometimes caustic and in any event fairly widespread criticism of the accord within the domestic constituencies of the democratic states of South Korea, Japan, and the United States. Disputes among NATO allies, as well as with others, over the best approach to take towards the civil war in Bosnia is yet a third case in point. The question is less one of conflicting interests than in competing prescriptions; the potential partners want the same thing, but they do not agree on how to get it.

COLLECTIVE ACTION

The problems just noted are compounded by the familiar dilemmas of collective action.[23] Even if all members of a coalition agree on who the main threat is *and* on how they should respond, their efforts to do so may be undermined by disagreements over who should run the risks and bear the costs of resistance. Because security is a collective good (once an adequate level of defense has been provided, all members of a coalition can "consume" it), weaker members of a coalition can ride free on the efforts of others, confident that others will protect them out of their own self-interest. The danger, of course, is that each member's efforts to pass the buck may lead the coalition to do too little to deter an adversary or to defeat them in war, even when it possesses greater overall resources. This problem clearly afflicted the coalitions against revolutionary France and Napoleon, whose members were constantly wrangling over subsidies, spoils, and strategy, and similar problems undermined the effort to balance against Hitler during the 1930s.[24] The familiar debates over burdensharing in NATO were another example of this problem, and U.S. complaints about the distribution of costs during the Gulf War eventually convinced Japan to make a sizable ($13 billion) financial contribution to the allied war effort.

As the latter two examples indicate, problems of collective action are not insurmountable. As discussed below, these problems will be less serious when there is a single dominant power who can afford to bear a disproportionate share of the burdens. When capabilities are more evenly distributed, however, the tendency to buck pass or ride free will be more pernicious. This does not bode well for a world that is increasingly dominated not by one or two but by several great powers.

THE PROBLEM OF UNCERTAINTY

A final obstacle to effective coalition performance is uncertainty. Inefficient balancing behavior is more likely when the threat is ambiguous, because it is much more difficult for states to agree on who the main threat is and on how they should respond. After the Bolshevik revolution, for example, British Prime Minister David Lloyd George argued against allied intervention by warning that the facts needed to make such a decision "had never been ascertained and were probably unascertainable."[25]   As noted earlier, it was difficult to form an effective coalition against Germany in part because the mediumpowers of Eastern Europe could not tell whether Nazi Germany or the Soviet Union posed the greater threat.   Similarly, Britain and France could not be completely sure until relatively late whether the main danger was Japan in the Far East, Italy in the Mediterranean, or Germany on the continent.   More recently, lack of information has plagued efforts to respond to the civil war in Bosnia, because potential coalition members disagreed about the circumstances in each case and could not obtain definitive information about current conditions, future intentions of various belligerents' leaders, or the likely consequences of alternative courses of action.   By contrast, Hitler's occupation of the rump of Czechoslovakia in March 1939 and Hussein's invasion of Kuwait in August 1990 removed all doubt about their aggressive aims and facilitated the formation of a countervailing coalition.

Uncertainty is a constant in world politics, of course, and the lack of perfect information is not an absolute barrier to forming an effective coalition.   On the whole, however, ambiguity about the nature or extent of the threat will make it more difficult to bring a coalition into being and will fuel disputes that undermine its efficiency.

Each of these obstacles is likely to decline as the level of threat increases.   As states become more threatening, the danger they pose will override other interests and permit states that are otherwise deeply suspicious to join forces, as the United States and Soviet Union did in World War II or as the United States and Syria did during the Gulf War. Similarly, disagreements over how to respond will decline as the threat becomes manifest, if only because a strategy of appeasement will be exposed as infeasible and containment (or war) will be seen as the only alternative.   The dilemmas of collective action will operate with less force when states are facing a truly grave threat, because victory will be more important than trying to maximize individual gains.   Finally, although truly dangerous powers may be able to disguise their ambitions for some time, they will not be able to hide them forever.   Thus, uncertainty about the level of threat will diminish over time, thereby facilitating the formation of a countervailing coalition.

These points suggest that coalitions will be most difficult to form in cases where there are several potential sources of threat and when the danger that each presents is ambiguous. The interests of potential members are more likely to conflict, their preferred strategies are more likely to differ, their desire to shift the burdens will be at its greatest, and their ability to resolve their differences by acquiring additional information will be low.   Unfortunately, these conditions are likely to predominate in the early 21st century, which means that forming and leading such coalitions will be more difficult in the future than it has been in the past.

4. STRUCTURES AND TRADEOFFS

All coalitions are not created equal, and the ability to assemble an effective coalition will also be affected by its *internal structure*. In particular, the dynamics of different coalitions will vary according to their *size, symmetry* and *degree of institutionalization*, leading to important strategic tradeoffs for prospective members.

SIZE

Napoleon Bonaparte once asked a rival diplomat, "How many allies do you have? Five? Ten? Twenty? The more you have, the better it is for me."[26] His remark illustrates a fundamental tradeoff between the size of a coalition and its likely effectiveness in war. Adding members increases the overall power available to the coalition, but it also intensifies the various obstacles to effective performance discussed above. As the number of members increases, their interests are more likely to conflict, achieving a consensus on strategy will be more difficult, and the temptation to ride free will be harder for each member to resist. Some coalition partners, while perhaps useful for political symbolism, can actually imperil the warfighting capabilities of a coalition. Senior military commanders of recent coalition operations, from the Gulf War to Somalia and Bosnia, testify to the dangers of indiscriminate coalition building.[27] Even among serious coalition partners, however, it will be difficult to satisfy each members' demands for compensation as the number of members grows and the inability to provide additional sidepayments will make it possible (or at least undesirable) to add new members even when they would strengthen the coalition.[28]

Several caveats should be noted at this point. By convincing potential aggressors that they will face overwhelming resistance, a large coalition may be more effective for purposes of deterrence, provided it does not become so large that its credibility suffers. Purely deterrent coalitions do not face the same problem of dividing future spoils that wartime coalitions do, though they will have to achieve some consensus on burdensharing and strategy if their deterrent threats are to be effective. Problems of alliance management will diminish if most members of the coalition are comparatively weak (at least relative to the alliance leader), especially if their participation is largely symbolic. For example, the Allied coalition in World War II eventually included more than two dozen states, but most of them were late arrivals who contributed little to the war effort and had little or no impact on policymaking among the "Big Three." The same lesson applies to the Gulf War; although some 35 states contributed to the United Nations coalition, the United States sent by far the largest contingent and dominated decisionmaking both before and during the war.[29] Although size always matters, its effects on the cohesion of a coalition will be greatest when the capabilities of the members are roughly equal.

SYMMETRY

A second element of coalition structure, the *degree of symmetry* among the members of a coalition, has two related but distinct dimensions. The first is the distribution of power within the coalition itself: is power equally distributed among the members or is it highly skewed? The second dimension concerns the *type* of capabilities that the different members possess; are they identical and interchangeable or are they different and complementary?

With respect to the first dimension, coalitions among roughly equal powers will face greater problems of internal management than coalitions where the distribution of power is unequal. In the latter case, the dominant power will be able to exercise greater leadership and the coalition is more likely to follow a coherent strategy. There is an obvious tradeoff here, however, insofar as greater unity and cohesion is achieved at the price of reduced overall capabilities. The dominant power might be able to do less if the other members were more capable, but it would have to pay more attention to their interests and the coalition would probably experience more severe internal rifts.

Among other things, this consideration explains why coalitions tend to be more stable and cohesive in a system marked by bipolarity. In a bipolar world, the two superpowers are less dependent on allied support and better able to manage the strains and tensions within their respective coalitions. In multipolarity, by contrast, the distribution of power within each coalition will be more equal and serious internal tensions will be more common.[30]

With regard to the second dimension, coalitions among states whose capabilities are different are likely to be more stable and efficient than coalitions among states whose assets are similar. The logic is essentially that of the division of labor; states with different but complementary capabilities can specialize in areas of relative advantage and create a coalition that is stronger than one where there is substantial duplication of effort.[31] During its imperial heyday, for example, Great Britain concentrated on maintaining its naval and financial power and formed coalitions with various land powers (exceptions, such as Japan, are notable for their distance from Great Britain), thereby achieving a more effective division of labor. Similarly, the United States was the world's supreme industrial power during World War II and provided the Grand Alliance with a mountain of materiel, while the Soviet Union provided the bulk of the manpower to defeat Nazi Germany.[32] A different type of division of labor arose during *Desert Storm;* the United States provided high-tech weaponry, airpower, intelligence, and most of the land forces, while Egypt and Syria gave the coalition greater legitimacy (given that the adversary was an Arab state) and Saudi Arabia provided the territory from which to prepare and launch the assault. When different states possess capabilities that their partners cannot easily duplicate, the stability of the resulting coalition will be enhanced.

DEGREE OF INSTITUTIONALIZATION

Coalitions also vary in terms of their *degree of institutionalization*. Once again, this aspect of internal structure takes two main forms. The first issue is the density of connections among potential partners prior to the decision to form the coalition. Such connections may include diplomatic relations, commercial relations, transnational contacts among influential elites, educational or military exchanges, and shared ethnic or historical ties. These links can help potential partners communicate their shared interests and coordinate their responses, thereby facilitating the formation of an effective strategic partnership.[33] A legacy of past cooperation will enhance these efforts as well, by making it easier for each partner to trust that the other will fulfill its pledges. When states do not enjoy a history of strategic cooperation and extensive contacts are absent, however, forming an effective coalition will be more difficult.[34] This consideration explains why great powers often provide military training to potential clients and also helps explain enduring associations like the U.S. relationship with Israel or the "special relationship" between the United States and England. By creating a favorable impression and promoting a shared world-view, these programs can cement an existing relationship or lay the foundation for a new one should it become desirable. As noted earlier, however, attempts to exploit these channels of influence in order to manipulate another state's behavior may provoke a hostile backlash and lead to an unexpected and undesirable rupture.[35]

Coalition Organization and Execution: Lessons Learned from the Gulf War

Our experience during the 1991 Gulf War indicates that a number of issues will affect how well the coalitions in which the United States is likely to participate will cohere and function:

- ❑ Precoalition groundwork. Advance preparation, such as increased joint training, education, exercises, and exchanges, can introduce U.S. Military personnel and civilian counterparts to prospective coalition partners.
- ❑ *Access to foreign facilities.* Because future coalitions are likely to be more flexible and short lived, the United States cannot count on the same degree of access to foreign military facilities that it enjoyed during the Cold War era. This suggests that U.S. Military forces will have to become more autonomous, even if achieving this capability is costly.
- ❑ *The core military group.* In any coalition, some countries inevitably become part of a core group while others remain peripheral to decisionmaking and the execution of operations. In *Desert Shield* and *Desert Storm,* the United States and Saudi Arabia were politically and financially at the core, whereas the United States, Britain, and perhaps France were militarily at the core. Combat operations will proceed more smoothly if core nations exclude those that cannot conduct combined operations with similar equipment and doctrine. On the periphery, there are two basic categories of partners: those that can make a useful contribution in the military operation and those that cannot, but add political cover.
- ❑ *Coalition maintenance.* A robust liaison with militarily and politically essential partners may be necessary to hold together a coalition. In the Gulf War, for instance, the United States saturated the Saudis' and other key partners' defense apparatuses with competent U.S. Civilians and officers to ensure a unity of effort. If combines combat operations are contemplated, then it is in the interest of U.S. Component commanders to check and double check, rehearse and re-rehearse actions to be undertaken to avoid costly mistakes, including fratricide. Given that coalitions are often symbolic and require much political give and take, U.S. Leaders may devote much effort to the collegiality and diplomacy required to placate the national sentiments of coalition partners.

The second issue is the degree of institutionalization within the coalition itself. At one extreme, formal alliances such as NATO can be highly institutionalized, with elaborate decisionmaking rules and an extensive bureaucratic apparatus.[36] At the other extreme, some coalitions (such as the Axis alliance in World War II or many inter-Arab coalitions) have been little more than *ad hoc* partnerships in which each member acted more or less independently. Highly institutionalized coalitions are more likely to endure once their original rationales are gone, which may help explain NATO's persistence following the collapse of the Soviet Union. High levels of institutionalization do not necessarily mean greater efficiency, however, depending on the specific arrangements that have developed. For example, NATO's anemic response to the Bosnian crisis suggests that formal decisionmaking procedures may provide a recipe for stalemate and inaction, especially when the different alliance members cannot agree on a common policy. Indeed, they may even provide a fig-leaf that various members can invoke to explain their inaction.

A STRATEGIC CHECKLIST

The preceding analysis has identified a number of issues that policymakers should consider when contemplating coalition warfare. The propositions set forth above suggest a series of questions that U.S. policymakers and strategic planners should consider when preparing a multilateral military response. This list does not provide definitive or precise policy guidance, but it does suggest where to look for it.

Sources of Threat

❏ Based on the different components of threat (power, proximity, offensive capabilities, intentions) which states or coalitions pose serious threat to U.S. interests, and what sorts of multilateral responses can help contain or alleviate the threat?

❏ Are other states similarly threatened? Are any other states especially vulnerable due to a shared border, ethnic irredenta, or an unresolved dispute? Do these potential partners harbor revisionist aims of their own, and are these aims compatible with U.S. interests?

❏ Do potential coalition members share U.S. goals and values, broadly defined? If not, is the threat sufficiently grave to warrant overlooking these considerations?

❏ Will the formation of a countervailing coalition deter the prospective aggressor, or is it more likely to provoke it? If the latter, how quickly can the coalition be brought into being and made militarily effective?
What compensation will have to be provided in order to cement the coalition? Alternatively, if the coalition is more important to our partners than it is to us, what sidepayments should we seek in exchange for our support?

Obstacles

❏ Do the prospective coalition members share our appraisal of the threat? Are differences a matter of degree, or do they regard the source of threat in a qualitatively different way?

❏ If the potential members of a coalition agree on the nature of the threat but disagree on how to respond to it, how might we convince them to accept our appraisal? Do we possess sufficient leverage to compel them to follow our lead? If not, can we afford to accept their recommendations in order to keep the coalition intact?

❏ What distribution of effort do we regard as fair and appropriate, based on the interests and capabilities of the coalition members? Is a formal or informal arrangement for distributing the costs and benefits of the coalition necessary and feasible?

❏ Are there any crucial items of information that would facilitate joint decisionmaking within the coalition? Can it be acquired?

Characteristics

❏ How large a coalition is needed? Is increasing the number of participants more likely to enhance its power and legitimacy, or will it merely dilute its cohesion and credibility?

❏ Are there any states with particular capabilities that would be especially valuable for dealing with this threat? If so, are there particular interests to which we can appeal in order to bring them into the coalition?

❏ Can we enlist any present or longstanding allies into the new coalition? Conversely, if the coalition would be improved by including a former adversary, what steps can we take to alleviate any lingering suspicions?

Although by no means complete, these questions provide a way to think through the formation and management of military coalitions. Providing specific answers to each one can help identify both prospective partners and identify the problems that may need to be overcome to create an effective coalition. Finally, these criteria also provide a guide to analyzing the politics of different regions in order to identify both potential threats and promising partners.

5. FORECASTING FUTURE COALITIONS

Because international conditions can change without warning, attempting to forecast the precise configuration of global military coalitions two decades from now is probably fruitless and possibly counterproductive. Indeed, because intentions are a central component of threat and may change with great rapidity, it will be extremely difficult to anticipate either the demand for future coalitions or their likely membership. After all, if we could not predict the end of the Cold War and cannot agree on the likelihood of future war, we are unlikely to achieve much consensus on who will ally with whom in 2015.

Effective future coalitions built over the next two decades almost surely will be builtaround some or all of America's current core allies. Yet while it seems quite plausible that the United States will retain close and valuable security relationships with majorEuropean and East Asian even 20 years from now, surely one cannot ignore thepossibility that dilemmas facing key U.S. alliances today may well lead to the dilution ordissolution of these potential wartime coalitions.* Consider the following current situation with respect to America's major multilateral alliance in Europe and its major bilateral alliance in Northeast Asia:

❑ *NATO:* In the mid-1990s, NATO remains the anchor of American engagement in Europe and the linchpin of transatlantic security. However, the most successful political-military alliance in modern history faces a number of crucial choices with regard to its future. Among these are the difficult issues associated with NATO's membership and mission. With regard to the former issue, the momentous challenge is to define the NATO-Russian relationship in a way that strengthens NATO, reassures the Central and Eastern European states, and satisfies Russia that its security is in no way diminished. With respect to the latter issue, the fundamental question is whether NATO will continue to be a collective defense alliance directed at outside threats, whether it will take on a different task as the provider of security to tall of Europe, including Russia, or whether its mission will be sufficiently manifest to justify its long-term survival at all.

❑ *The U.S.-Japan Alliance:* Throughout the Cold War, the U.S.-Japan security relationship was the cornerstone of American strategy in the Asia-Pacific region.

As the U.S.-Japan alliance enters the 21st century, however, it faces both enduring and new challenges to its effectiveness and existence. As long as Japan maintains a massive trade surplus wit the United States and a major threat fails to materialize, Americans increasingly will demand that the security relationship be leveraged to force Japan to make economic concessions. The find outcome of such a policy is unknown,but clearly it could run the risk of undermining the alliance. The demise of the alliance, in turn, could destabilize the increasingly important Asia-Pacific region, which lacks a mature regional security framework and remains marked by divided countries, territorial disputes, and historic suspicions.[37]

There is, however, no such things as a "foreseeable future." Rather than assuming that these security relationships will remain salient and coherent, it may be more useful simply to identify critical areas of certainty and uncertainty. What aspects of world politics can we safely anticipate, what aspects are most opaque, and what does each imply for U.S. strategic planning?[38]

CERTAINTIES

Perhaps the safest prediction one can make about the future international system is that it will be multipolar. Although some writers regard the present international system as "unipolar," with the United States as the sole surviving superpower, this condition is unlikely to endure for long. The decline of U.S. military power and the reemergence of other power centers will almost certainly create a situation where the U.S. is one of several great powers (even if it remains *primus inter pares* for some time).[39]

As suggested above, the return to multipolarity carries several important implications for future coalition strategies. The distribution of power is more equal in a multipolar world, which means that it will be more difficult to determine which states pose the greatest threats. As a result, international coalitions will be more flexible and less durable than they were during the Cold War. Moreover, because states balance against threats (and not just against power) how they evaluate each other's intentions will become more important as power becomes more evenly distributed. This tendency will place a greater premium on diplomatic skill and on compliance with prevailing international norms, and it will also increase the value of accurate assessments of other state's foreign policy agendas. The end of the Cold War will also increase the value of timely and accurate intelligence, because our assessments of what other states are up to will be critical to our ability to identify emerging threats and to forge effective responses.

Military coalitions will be more difficult to manage in multipolarity, because potential partners will have greater alliance options and will be less dependent on U.S. protection. This trend may also increase the danger of war by making it harder for coalition members to restrain aggressive or adventurous allies.[40] The problems of riding free and buckpassing will be more severe and aggressive powers will be tempted to exploit any inefficiencies in the balancing process. *Ominously, the demand for effective coalitions may be increasing just as our ability to create them is declining.*

A second area of certainty concerns the identity of the great powers. In the year 2015, a list of the world's great powers will certainly include the United States, Russia, and the People's Republic of China. The European Union will be on a par with these powers if unification continues, Germany will be a near-great power if the EU withers, and Japan will join the great power club if it further rearms (as it is likely to do). We can also be reasonably certain about the identity of potential medium powers: France, Great Britain and Italy are obvious candidates (unless they are part of a centralized European Union), along with India and Brazil. These states comprise the list of candidates for great and medium-power coalitions, and the configurations among them will largely determine the shape of the international system two decades from now.

Third, we can safely assume that the *rate of change* in world politics will continue to increase, at least with respect to the distribution of capabilities. In the past, major shifts in relative power emerged slowly, as the result of minor differences in long-term growth rates. At present, however, differences in national growth rates are substantially larger, which means that the balance of power (or threat) can change over a period of years rather than decades. This reinforces the conclusion that future coalitions will tend to be of shorter duration. Among other things, this possibility suggests that *U.S. strategic planning should seek to avoid excessive dependence on any particular ally.*

UNCERTAINTIES

There are at least four important areas of uncertainty that will exert a powerful effect on the demand for (and supply of) future coalitions. The first area is the international role of the United States. Although there is still a strong consensus for maintaining an active international presence, we should not underestimate the potential appeal of neo-isolationism. Historically, the United States has been willing to shoulder a major global role only in response to the threat of Eurasian hegemony, and the absence of a clear and compelling threat to U.S. interests will undoubtedly resurrect demands for retrenchment. This trend is already apparent in our declining defense capabilities and reluctance to use force in places like Bosnia, and the only question is how far this trend might go.

A second uncertainty concerns the possible spread of nuclear weapons. As the U.S. nuclear umbrella begins to fold, states such as Japan, South Korea, or Pakistan may be tempted to acquire a deterrent force of their own. A more worrisome possibility would be acquisition of nuclear weapons by revisionist states such as Iraq, Iran, or North Korea, especially given doubts about their ability to control whatever nuclear arsenals they might acquire.[41]

The possibility that several new states may seek to acquire nuclear weapons has several paradoxical implications for future coalitions. On the one hand, the desire to dampen pressure for proliferation will encourage current allies to extend security guarantees to other states as a means of diminishing their incentive to move ahead with their own nuclear programs. Moreover, one state's decision to acquire a nuclear arsenal is likely to alarm its neighbors and encourage them either to follow suit or to seek the protection of a nuclear-armed ally. In this sense, therefore, the possible spread of nuclear weapons will encourage coalitions to form. On the other hand, states that do acquire their own nuclear deterrent will have less need for allied support, which could make military coalitions somewhat *less* relevant.[42] Furthermore, *because nuclear weapons make it more difficult to take military action against states that possess them, their acquisition by other powers could further reduce the importance of military coalitions in anything but a purely defensive or deterrent role.*

Because acquiring a nuclear arsenal can be both economically and politically costly, it is difficult to forecast how rapid or widespread this trend might be. What one can say, however, is that the scope and spread of future proliferation will be an important part of the future strategic environment and is likely to have profound effects on future coalition possibilities.

A third question is the future of the former Soviet empire. Will democracy and capitalism finally take root in Russia and its former empire, or will the present (dis)order give way to some new form of authoritarianism? Will Russia join the West as peaceful status quo power or will it seek to restore its influence (if not its formal control) over much of its former empire? Will the civil and ethnic conflicts current raging there die down or escalate? The answers to these questions remain hotly debated and currently unknowable, and the answers that ultimately emerge will have far-reaching effects on the demand for future security coalitions (and on the willingness of other states to enter them).[43]

Finally, perhaps the most difficult factors to forecast are the likely *intentions* of the principal great powers, both because we lack good theories of how intentions are formed and because they are shaped both by each state's internal political processes and by the external environment in which it is placed. As suggested earlier, perceptions of intent will be especially important in shaping coalition choices in a multipolar world. In 2015, will we be facing a powerful, highly revisionist China seeking its own "sphere of influence" in East Asia, or a relatively benign China that is interested only in protecting its borders while concentrating on further economic development? Will Japan remain a quasipacifist state, or will it abandon the current limits on more active Japanese involvement in regional security affairs?[44] Will Germany remain strongly committed to the European idea and will its neighbors be willing to live with German predominance? Will "rogue states" like North Korea, Iraq or Iran multiply or dwindle? The answers to these question remain elusive as well, but are likely to play a powerful role in shaping future coalition choices. Among other things, this point suggests that the United States still has a powerful need for scholars with regional expertise, in order to provide the in-depth analysis that can help us gauge the intentions of foreign powers more accurately.

How these uncertainties are resolved will determine the need for military coalitions 20 years hence. If the U.S. remains available as an "offshore balancer," if liberalism takes firm root in the former Soviet Union, if the spread of nuclear weapons is confined to stable and satisfied powers with adequate safeguards and civilian control, and if rising powers do not acquire excessive ambitions along with their increased capabilities, then the world of 2015 will be fairly benign and the demand for military coalitions will be low. If all these factors are reversed, however, the danger of war will be considerable and the demand for allies will be correspondingly high. If it is still too early to predict which world we will face, it is not too early to look for warning signs and to ponder preventive measures.

6. CONCLUSION

The propositions developed above carry a number of obvious implications for U.S. foreign policy and grand strategy:

❏ *Although the end of the Cold War is permitting the United States to reduce its defense expenditures, the growing importance of coalition warfare implies that the United States should maintain an active diplomatic presence and reasonably robust defense capabilities.* It may be possible to assemble future coalitions "from scratch," but it will be easier to do so if we are already actively engaged with our potential partners and if we still possess capable military forces. Indeed, because advances in information-based warfare are likely to continue to accelerate in the coming decades, technologically-sophisticated partners may be increasingly hard to find.

❏ *Because future coalitions are likely to be more flexible and short-lived, the United States cannot count on the same degree of access to foreign military facilities that it enjoyed during the Cold War.* This possibility suggests that U.S. military forces will have to become more autonomous, even if achieving this capability is costly. Concomitantly and somewhat paradoxically, the United States may need to redouble its emphasis on combined readiness and interoperability with selected core allies with whom it shares deep and abiding common interests.

❏ *The United States should not take on widespread responsibilities of a "regional policeman" until it has made a careful assessment of the interests at stake and the likely costs of such a commitment.* At present, a number of states favor a continued (or expanded) U.S. military presence in the hope that this will dampen the possibility of renewed regional rivalries.[45] Such a policy may makes sense in some circumstances, but extending U.S. guarantees may be counterproductive if it encourages free riding, especially if the U.S. commitment is not especially firm. Indeed, perhaps the worst case would be a situation where a group of regional powers failed to respond to an emerging threat because they expected the United States to protect them, only to discover that we had concluded that our vital interests were not involved. Although it may be tempting to view a U.S. military presence as the best recipe for peace in Europe and Asia, this solution will not work for long if the United States is unwilling to act when serious challenges emerge. As always, our willingness to enter into military coalitions should be based on a careful assessment of U.S. interests and capabilities and the potential costs and benefits of each commitment.

❏ *One way for the U.S. to continue to assert its influence in regional or local crises and conflicts will be through vertical coalitions in which the United States provides information and information products and coalition partners field the troops and weapons.* Thus, in those conflicts in which U.S. vital interests are not at stake, the U.S. will want to have a hierarchical approach to which burdens it should or could bear. Moving from the lowest to the highest threshold of potential cost, the U.S. might wish to contribute: data from our robust network of sensors; software and systems integration to fuse both the data we provide and the data collected by the coalition partners, as well as simulation software for training and mission planning; the sensors themselves; weapons; and, finally, combat troops. Across the spectrum of potential conflicts, there are bound to be occasions when it is in the U.S. interest to be engaged but at a distance and then only indirectly; vertical coalitions may be appropriate, even welcome. On other occasions, however, vertical coalitions will be difficult to effect in practice, if it appears we are standing aloof from our friends in their hour of need.

❏ To *repeat a point made previously, the formation of future coalitions will heavily influenced by how states (including the United States) gauge each other's intentions, which means that domestic politics will play a greater role in our assessments of threat.* During the Cold War, perceptions of threat were largely determined by the distribution of world power and there was a remarkable consensus on who the main threats were and how we should respond. In the future, however, our evaluation of other countries will be more heavily influenced by their internal political condition, just as our own sense of strategic priorities will be determined less by the distribution of power than by the outcome of internal debates within the United States itself. This consideration highlights the need for regional expertise and accurate intelligence, to permit us to identify emerging threats early and to help us construct the consensus needed for an effective multilateral response.

Part III has focused on different aspects of military coalitions from the perspective of the United States. As such, we have implicitly assumed that the United States will remain a status quo power and that its primary objective in participating in military coalitions will be to enhance stability in general and to defend specific national interests in particular.

Most Americans are accustomed to viewing our foreign policy in similar terms; like most states, we tend to view our own behavior as benevolent and defensive—yet we should not assume that others will share this view. As the most powerful state in the international system, the United States will inevitably act in ways that impinge on other states' interests. Even governments we do not regard as hostile worry about the uses to which U.S. power might be put, and even our traditional friends may not see us as the good guys all the time. *This argument suggests that when thinking about future coalitions, we also need to think about* preventing *future coalitions from forming against us.* Although the threat we pose to others is reduced by our geographic distance from the other key centers of world power, it will still be advisable to use our power with restraint, so as not to appear needlessly threatening to others.

NOTES

1. During the Cold War, the United States and its allies controlled roughly two-thirds of gross world product, compared with less than one-fifth for the Soviet bloc. The Western alliance spent more each year on defense, had more men under arms, and (omitting China) had a larger combined population. See Stephen M. Walt, *The Origins of Alliances* (Ithaca: Cornell University Press, 1987), 274-81 and appendix II.

2. Examples include the realignments that followed the Iraqi, Iranian, Cuban, and Nicaraguan revolutions.

3. For example, most experts regard the Soviet-Egyptian Friendship Treaty of 1972 as a symptom of tensions between Cairo and Moscow rather than as evidence of a growing commitment.

4. This discussion is based on Walt, *Origins of Alliances*, and see also Stephen M. Walt, "Testing Theories of Alliance Formation: The Case of Southwest Asia," *International Organization* 43, no. 2 (1988); *Security Studies* 1, no. 3 (1992); "Multilateral Collective Security Arrangements," in Richard Shultz, Roy Godson and Ted Greenwood, eds., *Security Studies for the 1990s* (New York: Pergamon-Brassey's, 1993).

5. For classic expressions of this view, see Hans J. Morgenthau, *Politics Among Nations* (New York: Alfred A. Knopf, 1967); and Kenneth N. Waltz, *Theory of International Politics* (Reading: Addison-Wesley, 1978).

6. On the so-called power-distance gradient, see Kenneth Boulding, *Conflict and Defense: A General Theory* (New York: Harper Torchbooks, 1962) and Albert Wohlstetter, "Illusions of Distance," *Foreign Affairs* 46, no. 2 (1968).

7. See Kautilya, "Arthasastra," in Paul Seabury, ed., *Balance of Power* (San Francisco: Chandler Publishing, 1965).

8. See Walt, 158-65, 266; and also Steven David, *Choosing Sides: Alignment and Realignment in the Third World* (Baltimore: Johns Hopkins University Press, 1991). David uses the term "omnibalancing" to refer to the proclivity of developing-world leaders to seek alliances as an inoculation against *both* internal and external threats.

9. Stephen M. Walt, "Revolution and War," *World Politics* 44, no. 2 (1992).

10. David Garnham, "Explaining Middle Eastern Alignments during the Gulf War," *Jerusalem Journal of International Relations* 13, no. 3 (1991).

11. Eric Labs suggests that even weak states are reluctant to bandwagon, though they will do so as a last resort. See his "Do Weak States Bandwagon?" *Security Studies* 1, no. 3 (1992). See also Michael Handel, *Weak States in the International System* (London: Frank Cass, 1981); and Robert L. Rothstein, *Alliances and Small Powers* (New York: Columbia University Press, 1968).

12. Randall K. Schweller, "Bandwagoning for Profit: Bringing the Revisionist State Back In," *International Security* 19, no. 1 (1994).

13. For other examples, see Walt, "Testing Theories of Alliance Formation."

14. For this reason, partners in an offensive coalition are prone to quarrel once victory is achieved, often over the division of the spoils. Examples include the victorious coalition of Serbia, Bulgaria, Macedonia and Greece after the First Balkan War, or the Nazi-Soviet agreement to divide Poland in 1939.

15. For this reason (among others), present fears that the spread of Islamic fundamentalism might create a monolithic coalition of hostile, anti-Western states are greatly exaggerated. For contrary views, see Samuel P. Huntington, "The Clash of Civilizations?" *Foreign Affairs* 72, no. 3 (1993); and Judith Miller, "The Challenge of Radical Islam," *Foreign Affairs* 72, no. 2 (1993).

16. Paul Schroeder, "Alliances, 1815-1945: Weapons of Power or Tools of Management," in Klaus Knorr, ed., *Historical Dimensions of National Security Problems* (Lawrence, Kansas: University Press of Kansas, 1976).

17. See Walt, *Origins of Alliances*, 41-49 and chap. 7.

18. For a general discussion of these arrangements, see Robert Jervis, "Security Regimes," in Stephen Krasner, ed. *International Regimes* (Ithaca: Cornell University Press, 1983). An application of these ideas to post-Cold War Europe is Charles A. Kupchan and Clifford C. Kupchan, "Concerts, Collective Security, and the Future of Europe," *International Security* 16, no. 1 (1991); for critiques, see Richard K. Betts, "Systems for Peace or Causes of War: Collective Security, Arms Control, and the New Europe, *International Security* 17, no. 2 (1992); and John J. Mearsheimer, "The False Promise of International Institutions," *International Security* (forthcoming).

19. On these points, see Walt, "Alliances, Threats and U.S. Grand Strategy."

20. On the tensions within the first and second Coalitions, see John M. Sherwig, *Guineas and Gunpowder: British Foreign Aid in the Wars with France* (Cambridge, Mass.: 1969); Paul Schroeder, *The Transformation of European Politics* (Oxford: Clarendon Press, 1994); and Steven Ross, *European Diplomatic History, 1789-1815: France against Europe* (Garden City: Anchor Books, 1969), 87-92.

21. See John Thompson, *Russia, Bolshevism and the Versailles Peace* (Princeton: Princeton University Press, 1966), chap. 6.

22. One of the clearest signs of the Cold War's passing was Russia's willingness to support the UN action during the Gulf War, and its more recent willingness to endorse several proposals for ending the civil war in the former Yugoslavia.

23. The seminal work on this subject is Mancur Olson, *The Logic of Collective Action* (Cambridge, Mass.: Harvard University Press, 1965); and see also Mancur Olson and Richard Zeckhauser, "An Economic Theory of Alliances," *Review of Economics and Statistics* 48, no. 3 (1966).

24. On the French case, see Schroeder, *Transformation of European Politics*, "The Collapse of the Second Coalition," *Journal of Modern History* 59, no. 2 (1987); on the 1930s, see Barry Posen, *The Sources of Military Doctrine: France, Britain and Germany between the World Wars* (Ithaca: Cornell University Press, 1984), and Thomas J. Christensen and Jack Snyder, Chained Gangs and Passed Bucks: Predicting Alliance Patterns in Multipolarity," *International Organization* 44, no. 2 (1990).

25. Similarly, U.S. President Woodrow Wilson told a confidant that his impressions of Russia were based on "indefinite information," and his doubts helped convince him that the Allies should "leave it to the Russians to fight it out among themselves." Quoted in Richard H. Ullman, *Anglo-Soviet Relations, vol. 2: Britain and the Russian Civil War* (Princeton: Princeton University Press, 1968), 96-97; and Frederick S. Calhoun, *Power and Principle: Armed Intervention in Wilsonian Foreign Policy* (Kent, Ohio: Kent State University Press, 1986), 232, 238.

26. Quoted in Karl Roider, *Baron Thugut and Austria's Response to the French Revolution* (Princeton: Princeton University Press, 1987), 327.

27. On this general point, see Patrick M. Cronin, Conference on Standing-Up Coalitions, Washington, DC: National Defense University, March 1994.

28. For this reason, n-person game theory suggests that actors will tend to form "minimum winning coalitions." By making the coalition that is just large enough to win (but no larger) the members can maximize their own share of the spoils. See William Riker, *The Theory of Political Coalitions* (New Haven: Yale University Press, 1962).

29. See Lawrence Freeman and Ephraim Karsh, "How Kuwait Was Won: Strategy in the Gulf War," *International Security* 16, no. 2 (1991).

30. On the differing internal dynamics of bipolar and multipolar coalitions, see Glenn Snyder and Paul Diesing, *Conflict Among Nations: System Structure, Bargaining and Decisionmaking in International Crises* (Princeton: Princeton University Press, 1977), 419-29;"The Security Dilemma in Alliance Politics," *World Politics* 36, no. 4 (1984); and Snyder and Christensen, "Chained Gangs and Passed Bucks."

31. For an analysis of this point focusing on NATO, see Eliot A. Cohen, "NATO Standardization: The Perils of Common Sense," *Foreign Policy* no. 31 (1978).

32. On this point, see Paul F. Kennedy, *The Rise and Fall of British Naval Mastery* (London: Macmillan, 1976); and William McNeill, *America, Britain and Russia: Their Cooperation and Conflict 1941-46* (London: Oxford University Press, 1953).

33. For example, some commentators suggest that U.S. President George Bush was able to use his personal relations with other foreign leaders such as King Fahd of Saudi Arabia to bring the Gulf War coalition into being.

34. One reason for Rome's enduring hegemony in the ancient world may have been the difficulties its opponents faced in coordinating their responses. When a workable system of diplomatic communication emerged during the Renaissance, however, the prospects for European hegemony declined significantly. See Edward N. Luttwak, *The Grand Strategy of the Roman Empire* (Baltimore, Md: Johns Hopkins University Press, 1976), 92, 199-200; and Garret Mattingly, *Renaissance Diplomacy* (Boston, Mass.: Little, Brown and Co., 1971, chaps. 13-16.

35. An obvious example is Anwar Sadat's decision to expel his Soviet advisors and to realign with the United States, a decision at least partly based on Egyptian resentment over Soviet interference in Egyptian internal affairs. See Anwar el-Sadat, *In Search of Identity: An Autobiography* (New York: Harper and Row, 1977), 230-31; and Alvin Z. Rubinstein, *Red Star on the Nile: The Soviet-Egyptian Influence Relationship since the June War* (Princeton: Princeton University Press, 1976), 145-46 and passim.

36. See John S. Duffield, "International Regimes and Alliance Behavior: Explaining NATO Conventional Force Levels," *International Organization* 46, no. 4 (1992).

37. For a more detailed assessment of America's current security relationships, see Patrick M. Cronin, "Security Relationships and Overseas Presence," in Strategic *Assessment 1996: Instruments of U.S. Power* (Washington, DC: National Defense University Press, 1996), 109-126.

38. Recent efforts to forecast the future of world politics include John J. Mearsheimer, "Back to the Future: Instability in Europe after the Cold War," *International Security* 15, no. 1 (1990); Stephen Van Evera, "Primed for Peace: Europe after the Cold War," *International Security* 15, no. 3 (1990-91); Robert Jervis, "The Future of World Politics: Will It Resemble the Past?" *International Security* 16, no. 3 (1991-92) and Kenneth N. Waltz, 'The Emerging Structure of International Politics," *International Security* 18, no. 2 (1993).

39. On this point, see Christopher Layne, "The Unipolar Illusion: Why New Great Powers Will Rise," *International Security* 17, no. 4 (1993).

40. This is the "abandonment/entrapment" dilemma: because states will fear being isolated if their allies defect, they may be forced to support them and become entrapped in conflicts they would have preferred to avoid. See Snyder, "Security Dilemma in Alliance Politics."

41. See "The Proliferation Puzzle," a special issue of *Security Studies* 2, no. 3-4 (1993).

42. Indeed, other states will be reluctant to be too closely associated with some of the current candidates for the nuclear club, due to the fear of being dragged into dangerous confrontations by their nuclear armed allies.

43. See Vladimir P. Lukin, "Our Security Predicament," *Foreign Policy* no. 88 (1992) and Teresa Pelton Johnson and Steven E. Miller, eds., *Russian Security after the Cold War: Seven Views from Moscow* (Washington, D.C.: Brassey's, 1993). For an optimistic view, see Stephen Sestanovich, "Russia Turns the Corner, *Foreign Affairs* 73, no. 1 (1994); a more skeptical appraisal is Robert D. Blackwill and Sergei A. Karaganov, *Damage Limitation or Crisis: Russia and the Outside World* (Washington, D.C.: Brassey's, 1994), especially chap. 1.

44. For useful surveys of the security environment in Asia, see Aaron Friedberg, "Ripe for Rivalry: Prospects for Peace in a Multipolar Asia," and Richard K. Betts, "Wealth, Power and Instability: East Asia and the United States after the Cold War," *International Security* 18, no. 3 (1993-94).

45. For example, Poland, Ukraine and several other east European states have been clamoring for U.S. security guarantees and a number of East Asian states have expressed their desire for a continued U.S. military presence.

IV. TECHNOLOGY AND WARFARE

Martin C. Libicki is a Senior Fellow of the Advanced Command Technologies program, INSS, National Defense University. He is a specialist in the application of information technologies to national security issues. He has written extensively on information warfare, information technology standards, and the revolution in military affairs. Dr. Libicki received his doctorate in industrial economics from the University of California, Berkeley.

1. INTRODUCTION

Forecasts about tomorrow's battlefield depend on one's answer to a fundamental question: are the world's armed forces seeing a revolution in conventional military power driven by information technology? An answer first requires a clear definition of information-based warfare, a vision of the role technology plays in promoting military revolutions and an understanding of the changing rates at which improvements occur in the developmental cycle of a particular technology.

DEFINING INFORMATION-BASED WARFARE

Information-based warfare is that which utilizes information, especially computer-processed information, to impose one's will on an enemy. While all aspects of war are evolving rapidly, those driven by the computer-communications revolution are evolving the fastest. Thus, the description that follows of what warfare might be like in twenty years will concentrate on the changes in warfare wrought by the information revolution. This chapter considers technology holds—particularly information technology—to influence 21st warfare.

Information-based warfare's roots go back several decades. Already, the combined application of precision-guided munitions, long-range airborne and space-based sensors, and the development of tandem Global Positioning System and Inertial Navigation Systems (GPS/INS) guidance packages means that any target that can be located and identified can be engaged and disabled. These weapon systems have accentuated the importance of *hiding* and *seeking*. Over time, the offense will expend increasing effort seeking targets. After detection, their destruction will become ever more likely because of precision strike missiles. The defense will spend more resources on hiding, in camouflage, in trying to mimic background or civilian objects and in masking its signatures. The traditional warfare principles of firepower and maneuver may become far less relevant.

But other factors are also increasing the importance of information in warfare. These include command and control, mission planning, simulation, intelligence, and psychological operations. Each aspect of war is being transformed by the ever-greater speed and ever-lessening cost of collecting, processing,, and transmitting information.

WILL THE MTR BECOME AN RMA?

A Military-Technical Revolution (MTR) encompasses radical innovations in weapons or military equipment, and such technologies are or soon will be available on the world market, despite the present American lead in applications of information MTR,. American forces may be able to use such technology to gain a decisive advantage over their potential foes, but this will depend on whether they can employ the current MTR to initiate a Revolution in Military Affairs (RMA). An RMA results when a nation seizes an opportunity to transform its military doctrine, training, organization, equipment, tactics, operations and strategy in a coherent pattern in order to wage war in a novel and more effective manner. Examples of RMAs are the *levée en masse* of the revolutionary French Republic, the development of the *blitzkrieg* by the German Army and Air Force, and innovations in carrier warfare developed by the U.S. Navy. The underlying technologies utilized in all three RMAs were available to many countries at the time, but in each case only one country combined and employed them in a unique and successful manner to gain a decisive advantage in war.

The difficulty with predicting whether an RMA will emerge from the current MTR (and whether it will be ours or someone else's) originates in the search for a strategic rationale for an RMA. If the three examples above are indicative, an RMA emerges from a well-defined strategic problem. The *levée en masse,* for instance, was the response of Revolutionary France to invasion by the forces of the *ancien régime*. Military innovations carried out or proposed under the defunct Royal Army were wedded to the immense national energies unfettered by the revolution. The result was the huge French armies of unprecedented offensive power that smashed their way across Europe for 20 years. The Blitzkrieg permitted Germany to seize and hold the initiative and avoid the morass of slow-motion trench warfare. The U.S. Navy needed a method to conduct operations across the Earth's largest body of water.

Currently, the United States possesses the technology for a Revolution in Military Affairs, but it lacks a pressing strategic challenge to create one. Might the United States be motivated by the need to deter or defer a potential peer competitor? Such a problem does not necessarily have a military solution, nor is it generally viewed as an urgent priority. Would the United States look for innovative ways to wage war with minimal American casualties? Is the United States focused on figuring out how to project power without overseas bases, and, if so, is the RMA irrelevant to conflicts near existing bases? The more possible reasons one raises for an American RMA over the next 20 years, the less clear the focus becomes on a specific motivating challenge. Consequently, the likelihood of generating an American-led RMA from the information MTR remains highly uncertain. The only basis left for believing it will nevertheless take place is the generalized fear that complacency in its technological prowess will, more than any single factor, put United States armed forces at risk.

Will another country generate an RMA by 2015? Others may have clearer strategic objectives by the very nature of their geostrategic circumstances (e.g., the presence of so many potential great powers in the Asian Arc). However, if their most pressing challenge is to defeat a power much weaker than the United States, their response may be irrelevant to American concerns. Barring a direct military confrontation between the United States and a peer or near-peer competitor, the United States might confront an adversary facing two simultaneous strategic problems. Such an adversary might seek to defeat a local enemy at acceptable cost and also prevent or confound the intervention of the United States or another distant great power. Military units (e.g., massed tanks) that can do the first may be an easy conquest for our style of warfare. Military units that can do the latter (e.g., irregular units) may be unable to overcome conventional defenses at low cost. An even more difficult challenge to the United States would be provided by a state that used conventional force against local foes and threatened to use weapons of mass destruction to deter great power intervention. Consider the problem for the United States if Iraq had possessed nuclear capabilities in 1990 or if a nuclear-armed North Korea initiated a second war on the peninsula. Any U.S. response likely would combine counter-proliferation approaches with preemption, and even strategic deterrence, but this would hardly constitute an RMA.

CAVEATS OF MIDTERM FORECASTING

This report maintains that the emergence of a peer military competitor is not likely during the next 10 or 20 years, but it is considerably more likely after the year 2015. Under foreseeable circumstances, U.S. Armed Forces are likely to retain their present general superiority over those of any other state. However, they may not be invincible. It is possible that foreign forces may develop innovative ways of warfare that, at least temporarily, could grant them tactical or operational advantage. Even general American military superiority would not necessarily mean quick or easy victory in every case. We might suffer from other disadvantages, as well—we may be more sensitive to casualties, and we will almost certainly be farther from battlefields of 2015 than our potential foes. Furthermore, forecasting the degree of our superiority in a particular case requires knowledge of the military sophistication of a particular opponent. There is no way to know this in advance.

We can make some reasonable projections about the highest levels of military technological development in 20 years. To field a weapon system by 2015 would require the initiation of its development cycle by 2000 or so. Five years from now is barely time enough for a radically new invention to be proven and win the confidence necessary to justify a major development program. The capital replacement cycle for major weapons systems will also affect future inventories. For example, even if a new American tank program were initiated before 2000, it would not reach the field until roughly 2010. Barring accelerated procurement, such a hypothetical tank would account for only a low percentage of the Army's main battle tanks in 2015. To be sure, this example is not universally applicable. The upgrades that reify information warfare have faster development cycles. The Ballistic Missile Defense Organization (BMDO) has demonstrated that completely new equipment can be built in a 2-year cycle. A number of complex weapons systems, such as the airborne Joint Surveillance and Target Attack Radar System (JSTARS) have proven usable as early as 5 years prior to initial full operational capability. Nonetheless, most American and foreign equipment that would appear on the 2015 battlefield already exists or would be a recognizable development of existing systems.

Project 2015 starts with existing inventories, programs, and technologies and work forward 20 years to estimate how they might be used in the field and what opportunities they offer for doctrinal innovation. Yet, such forecasts require assessments of the likelihood and timing of technological advances. For instance, will the United States have, by 2015, a system capable of shooting down a tactical ballistic or a cruise missile (or a flock of them)? Assessing how well existing defensive systems can combat existing tactical ballistic missiles is hard enough, but predicting the relative course of two competing trend lines (better tracking/fuzing versus decreasing missile observability) involves even more uncertainties. The answers are critical because they affect the viability of a number of weapons platforms, such as surface ships. If the latter remain effective, certain operations, such as precision fire, may be best moved offshore. If no surface ships remain viable, the Navy will need to fundamentally rethink the way it contributes to warfare.

Such uncertainties about the future of warfare are increased by the growing importance of proliferation in determining the capabilities of whatever enemies we might face. Because the Soviet Union fundamentally armed itself from its own technological base (albeit with some purloined information), its likely progress could be debated within well-formed parameters. Proliferation regimes, however, extant and proposed, now cover a large variety of weaponry. Political decisions about how to extend current regimes, and under what circumstances they are observed, are difficult to foresee over a 20-year period. One even could assume that all currently fielded nonnuclear foreign weapons will be available on world markets sometime between now and 2015.

Predicting the range of results of information-based warfare is complicated further by the type of conflict involving such systems. When the order of battle was derived from learning the number of enemy divisions or battleships, the fundamental units for calculating opposing strength were visible and countable. As "hiding and seeking" becomes more important, however, enemy capabilities to see or be seen increasingly are being kept secret and are harder for us to divine. (Consider the secrecy with which we envelop the capabilities of our own spy satellites.) No foe will reveal beforehand how he intends to spoof our sensors. Indeed, we are unlikely to know the degree of his success at such measures, short of their employment.

RATES OF TECHNOLOGICAL DEVELOPMENT

The fundamental force driving the information revolution has been the rapid and consistent rate at which silicon-based devices have continued to improve. Between 1981, when IBM's original personal computer was introduced, to 1996 with today's 200MHz Pentium Pro machines, processor speeds for personal computers have risen several hundred-fold,, doubling every 2 years. The personal computer has had comparable increases in standard memory configurations (from 64,000 to 8,000,000 bytes), hard storage systems (from 10 megabytes in 1984 to the more common gigabytes today) and modem speeds (from 300 bits/second to 28,000 bits/second). In communications, phone-line trunk capacities have increased from 1.5 million bits per second to 155 million bits per second (using synchronous optical networks).

Such improvements in capacity will not cease—but will such rapid rates of change continue into the future, and how important will such improvements be? The answers lie in an understanding of the history of rates of development of particular technologies. Often the pattern has been an S-curve of slow-fast-slow improvement. For example, although the first commercial synthetic polymer, bakelite, was created in 1909, new polymer products initially entered the market slowly. Most of the major commodity polymers (plastics precursors) were commercialized in the 1950s and 1960s. After painfully slow development, the Germans and Italians flew the first successful jet-powered aircraft in 1939-1940. Led by British and American designs, jet engine performance improved radically between the mid-1940s and the mid-1960s. However, as these two examples illustrate, at some point, progress in the development of a technology slows. Although the range of available polymers or the capabilities of modern jet engines are both far greater than 25 years ago, these more recent advances have been of degree rather than of kind.

At the time of rapid development of a particular technology, hopes for such continued improvements extending indefinitely may seem reasonable. In retrospect, one can see that expectations had erred toward extreme optimism. As a result of past experience, most contemporary observers anticipate the same fate will befall information devices. Disagreement concentrates only on the question of when this slowdown will occur.

Another S-curve pattern illustrates the correlation of capabilities with underlying power. Early personal computers, for example, were poorly suited to word processing. They had 40-character screens and were so slow that typists were forced to pause while keystrokes were laboriously processed into text. Improvements followed rapidly, and increased speeds, hard disks, and spell-checking programs made word processing progressively easier to accomplish on computers. However, further improvements in computers are unlikely to alter the utility of computers for word processing. This provides another illustration of the fact that, after a certain point, even rapid changes in technology permit only modest increases in functionality.

Thus, as important to modern warfare as information capability has become, it now takes several orders of magnitude improvement to make a significant difference in capability. For example, a system capable of generating imagery accurate to the inch is not necessarily 144 times better than one capable of generating accuracy to the foot, even though the former reveals 144 times as much information, in the technical sense. This is not true for some other aspects of warfare. For example, tank guns that can be aimed accurately from 4,500 meters give overwhelming advantage to an armored force engaging an opponent with tanks armed with guns accurate to only 1,500 meters. In this case, the 3-to-1 superiority alone provides a decisive difference. The performance of Soviet tanks with their Iraqi crews in combat with their American counterparts in the Gulf War made that clear.

What do these two S-curve rates of technological development portend for American security? That depends on the stage of development. Let us suppose that the United States enjoys a 10-year lead in a certain area. If the technology were in its laboratory stage of development, it would provide the United States with little or no military advantage. After the technology was applied to military equipment, the 10-year advantage would provide the United States with a decisive advantage. However, after the rate of technological development slowed down for the United States, it would still be increasing at a rapid rate for the nearest American competitor. Our advantage would be considerably narrowed and eventually rendered relatively insignificant.

KEY QUESTIONS

In estimating the technology components of the national security environment in 2015, this chapter focusses on two questions. First, what will be the important differences between what American forces will be able to do then, compared to what they can do now? Second, what will be our advantages over our best potential military rival? While the capabilities of military systems adapted from commercial systems can be anticipated with a fair degree of certainty from expected developments in the latter field, the capabilities of purely military systems—a category which includes many sensors—are far harder to guess.

The primary source of uncertainty about future foreign military systems arises from difficulties determining the strategy for which they will be developed. Important new military capabilities are likely to be created by a relatively small number of foreign countries: more likely, the West Europeans, Russia and China; less likely, Japan and India;

perhaps some of the East Europeans, Korea, Taiwan, Israel, Brazil, and South Africa. On what strategic basis would they do so? Some may take advantage of American protection and seek to develop complementary capabilities. Others may orient their programs toward export sales.Yet others may concentrate on building capabilities against threats from the developing world. The answers to other questions are even harder to guess. Will suchcountries feel impelled to adapt to the information MTR or will they compete directly with capabilities that the United States will be demonstrating over the next twenty years? If the latter, will they be content to keep their innovations to themselves or, once they have mastered them, will they seek customers for such new technologies? What types of capabilities will the world's other advanced military powers pursue? A state that seeks to dominate its neighbors may develop conventional heavy weapons, but one that wishes to deter American involvement in a region may prefer lighter information-based systems. Without knowing the details of great-power rivalry in 2015, the easiest answers to these questions would arise from following commercial developments adapted to military use. Developments initiated by foreign militaries are far more difficult to foresee.

Finally, a distinction needs to be drawn between information-based warfare, the primary concentration of this chapter, and information warfare, a somewhat different topic. Although information warfare includes information-based warfare, it also includes other subtopics: the influence of information on national decisionmaking, and the conduct of conflict through non-violent attacks on computer systems, such as through viruses, worms, and "Trojan Horses." In addition, although information technologies can affect national security through other means—such as law enforcement against state-sponsored crime, struggle in the cultural-economic realm, and the formation and influence of transnational communities—this chapter does not discuss such subjects in order to avoid distraction from its focus on how progress in information technologies likely will improve the ability to prosecute warfare.

2. SYSTEMS TECHNOLOGIES

One way of looking at how technology might influence national security is to begin with the three great technical revolutions of our time: information, biology, and materials. All three result from the ability to microfabricate, that is, to manufacture on a scale as small as the atomic level. Microfabrication makes possible the creation of chips of greater speed and complexity, hence greater information-processing capacity. The ability to design and replicate complex biological molecules may permit increasingly sophisticated drugs and other medical treatments. The ability to build composites atom by atom may result in affordable and lightweight materials of extremely high strength and resilience.

Of these three revolutions, the information revolution is furthest advanced and thus most likely to influence the conduct of warfare 20 years hence. In time, biological and materials technology also may play a large role in warfare. For instance, the biological revolution may permit warriors to be psychologically or physiologically manipulated from afar. It may also permit the invention of terrible diseases to wreak havoc on mankind or nature. The materials revolution may enable the fabrication of armor far stronger and lighter than anything yet imagined. With biology and materials, however, such developments are speculative; capabilities imagined for more powerful compounds may be incompatible with physical laws. The information revolution, though, has actually occurred. True, it faces some scientific limits, such as a limited radio spectrum and chemical limits on battery power, but the world's militaries will face enormous challenges, as well as enjoy huge potential, over the next 20 years from innovations that already have been demonstrated and disseminated.

CAN THE VISIBLE BE KILLED?

The two fundamental issues of information-based warfare are:

❑ Can the visible be destroyed and, if so, under what conditions?

❑ What can be made visible and what can be kept hidden?

The development and refinement of Precision Guided Munitions (PGMs) suggests that anything that can be detected, classified, and assigned to a weapon can be destroyed. Many types of PGMs will soon be able to be guided to coordinates using GPS receivers, perhaps supplemented by INS guidance. The United States is fitting cruise missiles with such capabilities and also testing the Joint Direct Attack Munitions (JDAM), a completely new generation of PGMs with enhanced capabilities. GPS/INS guidance kits for Mk-82 bombs are already being installed for a few thousand dollars each; units under development in American laboratories ultimately may be available for below $1,000. Defense intelligence estimates have warned that countries such as Syria, Iran, India, or China will have GPS/INS-guided, low-observable missiles by 2000 or shortly thereafter.

Positional GPS/INS guidance retains two advantages over the self-contained sensor packages that currently guide PGMs.[1] First, it works against known targets with weak signatures or against targets with intermittent signatures, such as a sputtering radar. Secondly, positional guidance packages use far less artificial intelligence; thus, at some point in their development, they promise to be much less expensive than at present. Missiles so equipped could be made cheaply enough to use in overwhelming numbers in saturation attacks against high-value targets such as ships, command and control sites, and logistics facilities—but GPS updates to positional guidance systems would become dependent on the maintenance of communications with a central system. This creates a key vulnerability.

Three types of defense for visible objects are available: range/speed, armor/burial, and counterattack. Range helps to protect some of the more valuable American systems, such as the Airborne Warning and Control System (AWACS) and JSTARS, because they can operate while flying beyond the strike limits of current anti-air missiles. But these systems generate obvious signals and cannot maneuver very well to avoid missiles. Twenty years from now, they are likely to be more vulnerable to PGMs with the ranges of cruise missiles, although only a few countries are likely to have such PGMs. Even in 20 years, speed will protect reconnaissance aircraft and submarines against PGMs with limited speed and range.

Armor is likely to improve by 2015. However, barring a breakthrough in materials technology, armor will provide no panacea. The newest thinking on how to protect tanks is for its skin to react to information on an incoming round to shape itself and so blunt the missile's impact. Even if this approach succeeds in practice, however, it will be available for very few tanks by 2015. Furthermore, such armor may still be vulnerable to heavy weapons, fast penetrators, or saturation attacks. Burial and bunkering offer primitive but effective protection for command posts and stores, but such methods cannot protect moving targets. The United States has produced some bunker-busting bombs, but a truly effective nonnuclear burrowing bomb is unlikely to appear by 2015.

The Defense Department is funding generously the development of counterattack technologies to defend high-value targets against long-range missiles, but initial results have been mixed. In retrospect, the Patriot missile was not as successful in the Gulf War as initially believed. Upgraded and new defensive missiles both can appear impressive in one-on-one test engagements. But they will not insure against a determined saturation attack against a valuable target. Offensive missiles are also growing stealthier, making their intercept increasingly difficult. European missile manufacturers are reportedly applying radar-reducing finishes to their tactical missiles, such as the Penguin and FOG-M.

Target areas could also be defended by local electromagnetic pulse (EMP) or microwave burst to cripple the electronics on incoming missiles. But such defenses could be overcome by the use of older technologies such as mechanical fuzes or terminal trajectories. Counterelectronics weaponry could nevertheless be devised during the next decade that would confuse the systems on offensive missiles. Eventually, this could force the expensive replacement of many missile fuzes.

Over the next 20 years, certain characteristics of missiles are likely to evolve. Future missiles will be somewhat lighter and thus longer ranged than present models.[2] More missiles will be guided by fire-and-forget systems and armed with more sensitive target discrimination mechanisms. For special needs, such as the disabling of an installation with a high density of electronic systems, missile warheads could be armed with microwave-kill capabilities. Extremely long-range artillery could replace self-powered missiles for a number of tasks when effective elecromagnetic guns are developed.

In sum, by 2015, visibility is even more likely to equal death on the battlefield. Some American platforms will enjoy a high level of protection because of their stand-off range, armor, or self-defense systems. This would force our opponents to expend considerable ingenuity and resources if they wished to overcome our defenses. On the other hand, American forces will have high rates of success in destroying enemy targets after we detect them. Thus, the game of hide-and-seek will continue to grow in importance in clashes between conventional forces.

SEEKING AND HIDING

Seeking and hiding will determine the parameters of the battlespace of 2015. American abilities in these regards will be higher than that of those restricted to using only commercial or widely available military technologies. American detection capabilities will be determined by the performance of our sensors and integrators.

The purpose of sensing is to evaluate the battlespace environment for strategic, operational, and tactical purposes; the three tasks are interconnected. The integration of pieces of tactical information into a composite picture is a long-established intelligence method to assess a potential or actual opponent's strength and possible intentions. Awareness of the general situation, in turn, permits small-scale surveillance to focus on what is deemed particularly relevant. Modern sensor technology divides this latter task into a three-step process. One set of sensors indicates that an object justifies identification and tracking. Next, filters help focus on certain readings, to the exclusion of others. Finally, targets are pinpointed for prosecution. Often the last task is performed through yet other sensors. For the foreseeable future, synoptic pinpointing—finding targets by surveying everything at sufficiently high resolution—is unlikely to be possible except under very specialized conditions. Nonetheless, by 2015, some combination of sufficiently powerful computers and discriminating filters may automate a large share of what is currently accomplished only by human intelligence. The United States is likely to lead in such applications, but even our systems will tend to find only what they are looking for where they are programmed to look.

Sensors can be divided into two categories: stand-off systems that operate from space or the sea, and intrusive systems that operate from the air and the ground. The farther away a sensor operates from enemy-controlled area, the more survivable it is and the easier to deploy in circumstances short of war, or where the United States is not directly involved. Sensor employment is also influenced by the concept of plausible deniability. A high-flying reconnaissance aircraft can be used in peacetime without diplomatic risk only if it can avoid coming down in the territory it is observing. Similarly, a sensor that cannot be traced has greater political potential for use than one with an obvious national origin. By 2015, American forces may also have access to the information that states are routinely collecting by sensors monitoring their own activities, such as airport or seaport operations. Such access would be expected to fall off as international tensions mounted.

SPACE-BASED SENSORS

There are two types of current satellite surveillance systems: low-earth orbit and geosynchronous. Low-earth orbit satellites can take detailed pictures in the visible, infrared, and microwave bands, using Synthetic Aperture Radar (SAR). Such satellites can stay over one point for only a few minutes and can return only every few days. The tactical employment of such satellites is limited further because their flight schedules provide knowledge of surveillance times to those wishing to hide or cease activities during those periods. Geosynchronous satellites, used to scan most of a hemisphere, can provide continuous observation of specific spots, but they provide poor image resolution from their 35,000-kilometer-high orbits. Geosynchronous satellites generally are used for electronic intelligence and to search for infrared signatures of ballistic missiles. As surveillance satellites are adapted for tactical and operational, rather than strategic, use, placing them in medium-earth orbits may permit the combination of adequate resolution and continuous observation capabilities. If four Hubble-class sensors were placed in a 7,000-kilometer-high equatorial orbit, they could observe most points between 60 degrees north and south with a 2-meter resolution.[3] Molniya orbits (north-south elliptical) also have some advantages if the area of interest is limited, such as the Northern Hemisphere.

Alternatively, the success of the Ballistic Missiles Defense Organization's multiple-sensor technology integration (MSTI) and Clementine spacecraft suggests that inexpensive light satellites can provide adequate resolution in low-earth orbits. Each cost roughly $30 to $50 million, had multiple sensors, weighed roughly a kilogram in weight and was capable of image resolution down to 20 meters.[4] A sufficiently large fleet of such satellites with software-linked sensors from many different sources could keep any one location under near-constant surveillance. Using many of such satellites to look at a single point would render useless attempts at hiding from observation.

While the United States is currently more advanced than other countries in building surveillance satellites, how secure is that lead? Russia and France are not far behind in sophistication, and. China and Japan are catching up. By 2015, India (whose IRS satellites have fairly advanced sensors), Israel, Korea, and Canada also may have made significant advances. Several satellites that were designed for environmental monitoring already work at the 20-meter resolution level and the possible proliferation of a 1-meter resolution capability is not unimaginable. After all, at present, three American companies are vying to sell 1-meter systems on the world market. By 2005, France, Russia, and perhaps Japan may possess such satellite capabilities.

By 2015, commercially available satellites will have capabilities close to those of contemporary American military satellites. Obviously, military usefulness would be greatly enhanced by the delivery of images faster than even American satellites can now provide;

current image-processing times from many American systems limit military responses to transient data. American forces have recently arranged to receive real-time data from France's Spot satellite. Indeed, military use of third-party satellites, even those configured for environmental purposes, will rise substantially over the next 20 years.

A significant reduction in the cost of lifting a kilogram into low-earth orbit could allow far more orbital and suborbital launches by 2015. Currently the lowest cost—using payloads of 10 metric tons or more—is roughly $10,000 per kilogram ($20,000 per for small payloads). Although, several aerospace contractors tout reusable launch vehicles that could cut this cost to perhaps $1,000 a kilogram, [5] how well grounded are these estimates? The Space Shuttle originally was predicated on low costs and frequent launches but resulted in few economies relative to older technologies. Still, some aerospace engineers claim that reusable launch vehicles (of which single-stage-to-orbit are one type) could become available in 10 years if the U.S. Government chose one and invested as little as $4 billion in its development. More conservatively, NASA has estimated it would require 25 years and $20 billion. Meanwhile, Orbital Sciences Corporation, the world leader in light launchers, is striving to reuse 75 percent of its rocket components. If successful, its per-kilogram launch costs could be as little as $5,000 for small, individually launched payloads.

Might American manufacturers alone be able to cut launch costs by such large margins? It is unlikely that the other major space-faring countries—by 2015, Russia, France, China, Japan and perhaps India—would permit the United States to maintain such advantage. As followers, their research and development path to cheap space transport will be substantially reduced by learning from American successes and failures. One can assume that it would take them about 10 years from when the first U.S. reusable launch system appeared to possess the same capability themselves.

What would substantially cheaper access to space imply for American national security? Lower launch costs might increase the number of satellites in orbit, but how much it would do so would depend on whether the freedom to make satellites heavier would equate to making them cheaper. Other factors would keep the population of satellites under control, such as limited spectrum or geosynchronous "parking spaces". Conversely, very cheap space launch costs might enable the creation of buckshot-style antisatellite systems.

The largest single military result of lower launch costs might be cheaper ordnance delivery. A cost of a $10,000-per-kilogram launch to low-earth orbit means, in theory, that a 200-kilogram bomb (e.g., a Mk-82) could be dropped on any location on earth for $2 million. Still, this price is only barely competitive with a cruise-missile delivery. Military effectiveness of low-orbit ordnance delivery also would require surmounting other obstacles: the lead times for launch preparation, the cost of keeping a rocket on the launch pad long enough for sufficient target opportunities to justify a cost-effective ordnance payload, the potential for confusing a conventional launch for a ballistic missile attack, vulnerabilities to space-based lasers, and plasma plumes that could limit midcourse corrections on missiles as they reenter the atmosphere.

If the $2 million launch cost were $200,000, however, the number of targets that could be allocated cost effectively to such rockets would be very large. By 2015, if reusable spacecraft are cheap, easy and quick to launch (particularly if they are untethered from fixed-launch facilities), range could greatly diminish as a factor in heavy conventional warfare. Of course one has to consider current treaty restrictions against space-based weaponry and fractional orbital bombardment systems, as well as limits on the number of strategic rockets and on the range of tactical rockets.

NAVAL SYSTEMS

Unless a rivalry develops between two great naval powers, the next 20 years are unlikely to produce dramatic improvements in deep-ocean nuclear submarine technology. Instead, underwater technology developments will focus on shallow-water capabilities and nonnuclear boats, particularly those driven by air-independent fuel-cell systems. Nonnuclear boat designs are producing quieter submarines and ones capable of longer sustained operations. The proliferation of small attack submarines of European design is likely to make littoral operations increasingly risky. Even so, the current generation of submarines in developing-world navies is below the technology level at which the U.S. Navy can honestly profess great concern. But the prospective improvement in the next generation of European designs—and the likelihood of equally sophisticated Asian-designed submarines appearing—suggests that the U.S. Navy will have some cause for worry from both the quality and numbers of nonnuclear foreign submarines by 2015.

By 2015, mine warfare is likely to pose graver risks to large warships operating near shore and in shallow waters. Although not a widely reported fact, antiship mines caused more damage to allied warships in the Gulf War than any of the other more highly publicized systems. Future shallow-water mines (e.g., plastic mines) are likely to be increasingly difficult to detect and defeat, particularly if they are cued by independent sensor systems. Those who design such mines will strive to give them the acoustic signature of rocks. Their true character would be revealed only when fired. At that point, they would take on the characteristics of torpedoes, capable of sinking even the largest ships when used in concentration. The only impediment to the increasing sophistication of mines over the next 20 years is that most Western countries—with the exception of Italy—are not pressing the development of such technology. Advances are more likely to come from developing-world maritime states.

Naval systems used as sensors have certain advantages. They can be legally deployed prior to engagement. Standing offshore, they can pick up electronic intelligence and, through acoustic sensors, can monitor port operations. They can oversee the flight operations of coastal cities, peer into mountainous terrain and, from some locations, acquire radar signatures that hug the earth. These functions do have limits. For example, line-of-sight needs require naval sensors to be 30-meters high to observe the closest shoreline or small vessels in harbor at a distance of some 20 kilometers offshore.

Nevertheless, by 2015, bringing a large ship to within 20 kilometers of another nation's coastline to monitor activities may be both risky and inefficient. Risk would come from being a visible target within range of many land-based systems. Inefficiency would result from the limited range of any single platform. Still, naval air launched from a single platform would extend the observation coverage the platform could provide by an order of magnitude. But inefficiency also would stem from the difficulty of sustaining operations for any length of time without rotating ships. Generally, three ships are required to keep one on station indefinitely, but for some areas remote from North America, such as the Indian Ocean, this figure may be closer to five-to-one for sustained American naval operations. Thus, a series of buoys, possibly complemented by unmanned aerial vehicles

(UAVs), might prove far more efficient at collecting signatures. Buoys do not stand as tall as ships but, in sufficient combination, might offer a radar "dish" of sufficient strength to simulate effectively today's land-based, over-the-horizon backscatter radars. Distributed buoys would have to pass large quantities of data back and forth to form a coherent picture. Still, by 2015, such a capability could be possible with enough improvements in computing power.

A future variant on the acoustic naval sensor may be the seismic sensor that detects otherwise inaccessible vibrations caused by surface movement of large vehicles. It would take considerable practice before such signals could be translated into comprehensible patterns. As with offshore buoys, large numbers of sensors coordinated with high-bandwidth links and plenty of exercises would be required before usable information routinely could be expected to be collected from such systems.

AIRBORNE SENSORS

Unmanned aerial vehicles are the subject of a number of Defense Department programs aimed at the creation of many different types for a wide array of missions. Although they set the standards for endurance and capabilities, 30 other countries also make UAVs of varying degrees of sophistication (e.g., in terms of sensor package, system integration and platform stealthiness). As a result, the United States does not have the overwhelming lead in this technology that it possesses in space sensors. UAVs function much closer to a given surveillance area than satellites can. Thus, a sensor package on a satellite with a 10-meter resolution can offer a 0.1-meter resolution when mounted on a UAV. Of course, the field of view from a UAV also is far smaller. But UAVs enjoy the enormous advantage over space-based optical sensors of being able to operate under cloud cover. Given their special capabilities, UAV sensors can identify an object, when sensors on a satellite can only spot it.

However, UAVs have great disadvantages. Because they violate airspace, they can create political problems when flown in other than wartime circumstances. UAVs are manpower intensive to operate and require that operators be within relatively close range of the battlefield. If spotted, UAVs can be blinded or destroyed. While UAVs can be stealthier than aircraft when flown at night, they are far more observable by day, and the air turbulence they create also may reveal their presence. Unlike stealth aircraft, UAVs are useless if not communicating. Since most UAV communication is through imagery, they need to use fairly high-power, high-bandwidth channels for transmission. This increases the risk of their detection. Alternatively, UAVs can carry film cameras, but that delays the delivery of useful imagery. Current acquisition doctrine seems to favor long loitering times and high levels of stealth. Both increase UAV costs. An alternative doctrine of many, cheap, short-loiter UAVs may prove preferable.

GROUND-BASED SENSORS

Within the next 20 years ground-based sensors are likely to be greatly improved. Ground-based sensors would be useful for picking up signatures carried through the atmosphere, notably sound and vapors. For example, a bomber flying low to evade radar may leave a very distinct signature pattern among densely placed acoustic sensors.

Very sensitive chemical sensors are under active development for civilian and military purposes alike. "Sniffers" could detect the presence of human soldiers, as well as the emissions of mechanical objects. The movement of metal objects can also be detected through their effect on magnetic fields (in the same way that stop lights are prepped by vehicle movements). Gravimetric sensors are being developed to differentiate among passing vehicles such as empty, lightly loaded or densely packed trucks.

Long-range and short-range sensors will require different deployment doctrines. Short-range sensors can only provide wide area coverage if they are employed in large numbers. Thus, they must be inexpensive to be cost-effective. Adequate resolution, such as for triangulation of signature sources, requires they be networked in real time. Short-range sensors will work best as adjuncts to other sensors, for confirmation and for complicating the work of opponents charged with eliminating offensive signatures.

The human senses coupled to the human brain provide the best ground-based sensor. The soldier of 2015 is likely to be equipped with a portable supercomputer, coupled with digital radio-based communications capable of relatively reliable video data exchange. Such a soldier could conceivably navigate with high-resolution, near-real-time photographic maps, perhaps linked with portable expert systems and might even operate using systems capable of simulating alternative courses of action, allowing the evaluation of possible consequences in advance.

INTEGRATION

It is one thing to gather all sorts of signature information about the battlefield; it is quite another to integrate such information into a coherent picture. Systems integration has gained a notorious reputation for taking longer and working more poorly than previously planned. Many weapon systems, for instance, carry electronics whose system parameters had to be frozen (and thus grew obsolescent) over the many years required to tie all the subsystems together.

Systems integration may fare better in the future than we have a right to believe. Substantial progress has been made in understanding the problems of systems integration. Data fusion, an application which puts great pressure on systems integration, is recognized as a skill that must be mastered to survive on the future battlefield. The great value of reliable software was emphasized by the controversy over the Strategic Defense Initiative. A mix of open-systems design philosophy, object-oriented programming, megaprogramming, tools integration, and Computer Assisted Software Engineering (CASE) may generate reliable techniques for managing complexity. Although the American defense industry base is being severely reduced, a large number of American defense-oriented systems personnel may be able to exercise their talents in nondefense projects. These range from designing public infrastructure, such as intelligent vehicle and highways, and earth observation, to intelligent manufacturing, and outfitting the global information infrastructure. Simulation is evolving into a technology through which systems integration concepts can be tested. Finally, the American armed forces are beginning to understand how the failure to interwork information systems from the various warfighting communities hinders the exploitation of the information collected. Continued emphasis on supporting joint and combined operations puts pressure on each service to exchange information with the rest.

The United States is likely to remain the world leader in systems engineering, as indicated by its substantial lead in software exports. A conservative estimate is that the United States will retain a modest advantage over Europe, a notable lead over Japan, and a wide edge over the three other potential great powers: Russia, China, and India. These advantages, however, will be most evident only with very large, world-class systems. Foreign countries are rapidly improving their software capabilities, whether measured in terms of software maturity or clever algorithms. To the extent that useful military systems can be constructed with medium-scale software, American advantages could be less significant by 2015 than at present.

Nonetheless, to a great extent, systems integration can be purchased abroad rather than developed at home. A country does not need an extensive higher educational infrastructure for that purpose if the graduate schools of the United States can educate that state's engineering elite. More than half of engineering doctorates awarded in this country are conferred on non-Americans, most from developing countries. While some remain and strengthen American society, most eventually return home.

Similarly, a nation can buy systems integration technology through purchase of an entire complex. Examples include highly sophisticated process control machinery (e.g., a modern refinery) or air traffic control systems, which resemble tomorrow's command-and-control systems. In 10 to 20 years, countries may be purchasing even more sophisticated energy complexes. A country's engineers may be able to decrypt the techniques that make systems integration work at the highest level. After that, if they could match the software and the successively lower levels of aggregation, they could acquire a total systems expertise almost at American levels. Brazil's $1.5 billion Amazon monitoring contract, recently won by Raytheon, may be a prototype of a system that can monitor a nation's entire defense zone.

COMMERCIAL CAPABILITIES

It would be very difficult to maintain the distinct American advantage in information-based warfare over the next 20 years. The relevant technologies are decreasingly the products of classified military-industrial complexes and increasingly the products of the commercial marketplace. Over the next 10 years, a sophisticated opponent will be able to buy or lease a wide panoply of capabilities from around the world: in GPS, surveillance, communications, direct broadcast, systems integration, internetworking, cryptography, and air-based imaging. Furthermore, the costs of such purchases will progressively decrease. While the U.S. military still may enjoy a lead in each of these areas of information-based warfare, our lead may have decreased considerably compared to 1995 Despite having been purchased at a large cost multiple.

For example, GPS is now universally available. Signals can be received by devices costing a few hundred dollars. In theory, the American military could degrade GPS signals so that our forces could determine locations far more closely that our adversaries, limited to 100 meter accuracies, can. In practice, three factors militate against this safeguard. First, the U.S. Government has promoted the use of GPS for civilian purposes, most notably commercial aviation. Only a major and prolonged crisis could justify the global degradation of information that we have persuaded others to rely upon for their safety.[6] But accurate GPS data could enable a rocket attack against U.S. forces deployed in smaller contingencies. Since U.S. forces have access to the classified GPS signal, we might find it useful to jam the unclassified signal locally, but this is no panacea either. Second, GPS may be complemented by other navigation systems, such as Glonass and future additions to the Inmarsat and other communications constellations. Europeans are mulling the value of their own navigational capabilities. Third, the development of differential GPS means that if a set of fixed points near a target can be ascertained with precision, the target can be located with similar precision. Differential GPS systems are likely to proliferate throughout North America, Europe, and East Asia by 2000. Their accuracy exceeds that of Military Specification systems without differential correction.

GPS coupled with sufficiently good surveillance data theoretically places virtually every fixed facility at risk. Although U.S. forces employ camouflage and other deceptive tactics for many field installations, most logistics dumps, barracks, and command headquarters cannot be well hidden. Many such facilities could be identified and located if someone knew their general vicinity. In fact, if the facility were public, a terrorist with a portable GPS device would suffice to target it.

Overhead surveillance can locate fixed facilities with accuracy to within a meter or two. At present, the United States and the Russians alone can perform such detailed surveillance, but with the fall of the Soviet Union, a vigorous market has developed in Russian 2-meter imagery. The decision to permit sales of one-meter imagery from U.S. satellites would present any government or terrorist organization with the ability to collect a considerable volume of intelligence (until the United States exercises its prerogative of shutting it off). Over the next 20 years, the sale of satellites with such capabilities would permit many countries to acquire and transmit such imagery in near-real time. The obvious advantages offered by imagery to our forces in the Gulf War have prompted many states to consider acquiring better surveillance satellites, notably the French, the Gulf states, and the Japanese—the latter under the cover of disaster monitoring.

Another rapidly burgeoning information-gathering capability flows from the use of digital video cameras mounted on UAVs. For the last 10 years, an American company has been exporting digital-imaging systems that can collect high-resolution imagery 50 miles to each side with real-time data-links to ground locations. Video cameras are inexpensive, but the resolution of the mid-1990s (just under 300 lines) is relatively imprecise. The advent of high-definition television will create a market for high-resolution cameras, offering two-to-three times the line density. Their digitization will certainly take place by 2015. Electronic still cameras have been slow coming to market but they are already being sold and thier popularity should rise sharply within 10 years. Digital cellular telephony is already available through several technologies. By 2015 it will be both ubiquitous and capable of sufficiently high bandwidth to transmit imagery directly. Any number of Asian companies will make them commercially available.

American forces might attempt to deny an enemy such communications capability by blocking access to third-party satellites, but such an attempt could present several problems of a political nature. If every satellite owner were to cooperate, then access by our opponent to satellite links might be blocked, but what if cooperation were denied? Jamming signals to and from geosynchronous satellites frequently requires being in the line of sight. Global low-earth-orbit cellular systems would make it even more difficult to deny communications. A system's managers could refuse to transmit signals into and out of a region but doing so would eliminate service for nonbelligerent neighboring states. Jamming signals also could limit local use of global cellular systems However, it could be very difficult to shut down a system used by irregular forces operating inside a friendly country or to interrupt a primitive command and control system based on citizen's band radio. Similar difficulties would arise in interrupting another nation's air traffic control network without also interfering with international air traffic control operations in the general vicinity.

The rapid expansion of cellular communications may complicate targeting even further. At present, cellular systems use mobile terminals but fixed switches. The latter can be targeted easily. Yet, as electronic components continue to be reduced in size, future switches may themselves become mobile. Already, the development of personal communication systems points in this direction. One American company has managed to put the electronics for a modest-size cellular switch inside a large briefcase. The smaller the cell, the less power is required to operate it and the smaller its electronic signature. Thus, by 2015, some nodes may be virtually impossible to find and target.

Even without sensor proliferation, increasing global communications connectivity will decrease the chances for military activity to occur unnoticed. The daylight movement of an infantry platoon past a village can be kept secret from those outside the area if it is not connected electronically with the wider world. But as developing-world hinterlands become tied into the global communications network, such movements are more apt to be reported. Indeed, the marriage of digital video cameras with digital cellular, the products of which should be widespread throughout the Americas and Eurasia by 2015, means that many military movements are potentially liable to detection.

Direct broadcast satellite (DBS) television satellites may become ubiquitous in most areas of the developing world over the next decade. Most such satellites broadcasts reach several countries at once. Thus, jamming a particular channel would entail international complications. Again, unless the ownership of these satellites is heavily concentrated, some owner likely would be willing to provide television signals for even international outlaw states.

The Internet provides another broad conduit of data. An enemy that has retained phone connections can retain Internet service and thus the ability to broadcast messages internationally. As electronic commerce moves onto the Net, even a country facing an "information blockade" could get its software cast into a chip in any one of the world's many silicon foundries. More generally, the ubiquity of Internet connections makes it easier to acquire the world's knowledge of unclassified technical information.

What prevents the United States from destroying an opponent's space systems? One obstacle would be presented by an enemy using a third party's satellites. Unless every country with surveillance capability agrees not to sell its imagery, a route from neutral satellites to recipients hostile to the United States would not be difficult to create. In the Gulf War, it was sufficient to reach agreement with Russia to protect our "left hook" maneuver into Iraq from being reported to Baghdad. But with every passing year there will more satellite operators, making such embargoes increasingly difficult to maintain. Moreover, we may not always be in conflict with a pariah state like Iraq. Ostensibly neutral powers may surreptitiously help our opponent. The same logic applies to communications satellites. Unless every transponder's owner is careful to avoid uplinks from our foes, transmission will occur. And there are more than 1,000 transponders within sight of every point on the globe. The United States could demand positive proof that the owners of every possible space system is cooperating with us and destroy the satellites of those who refuse—but would we be willing to enforce this dictum in any conflict short of a global war?

HIDING

Although the balance between hiders and seekers is likely to tilt towards seekers, hiders also will be able to take advantage of new technologies such as stealth. Successive generations of U.S. equipment will incorporate increasing degrees of stealth; this is already true in regard to high performance aircraft and submarines. Stealth principles are being extended even to helicopters, certain surface ship classes and even to tanks. Current techniques include radar-absorbing materials, specially crafted surfaces, and false signal generators. Soon, noise-suppressing devices, the kind being engineered for vacuum cleaners, will be added to the stealth armory. Although the United States enjoys a strong lead in the area, component technologies already are understood in Europe, Russia and Japan.

Stealth, however, is no panacea. Many platforms use stealth not to hide but to delay detection, lowering their exposure time beneath the enemy engagement cycle. Information technologies are reducing the period required to engage a target, however, as sensors of increasing variety, number, and acuity appear, the cost of achieving a given level of stealthiness will increase. It take considerable maintenance to keep stealth aircraft stealthy. The more expensive the platform the fewer can be bought, the more they need to be protected, the stealthier and more complex they become, and so on. By 2015 the types of platforms that can made stealthy in a cost-effective manner may be roughly the same as they are in 1995: submarines, night-attack aircraft, and certain special operations forces equipment.

Other methods of hiding are operational: the proper employment of force elements, taking advantage of terrain, darkness and weather, and the use of decoys and camouflage. Operational and tactical adaptations to ever-improving and proliferating sensors, and the way sensors will be employed, are difficult to anticipate. Success against sensors will vary by national doctrine, and even from unit to unit. Electronic decoys designed to disguise force concentrations may be employed at the tactical, operational, and strategic level.[7] But platform decoys are likely to degenerate in effectiveness as sensors improve. Decoys for smaller weapons and sensors may increase in utility by 2015.

Another opeational route to stealth is to disguise military platforms as commercial ones. Thus trucks could be used to carry missiles, merchant ships could host hidden naval guns, and bombings could be carried out by wide-bodied aircraft. As information processing elements become smaller, they can more easily fit within such platforms without distorting their shapes into distinctly recognizable profiles. An enemy whose assets are so hidden forces the other side to target assets not exclusively by signature but by more operational attributes (e.g., any truck here must be up to no good). In the end, the enemy must engage far more targets, but at the risk of blurring the distinction between what is and is not considered fair game. The more bombs, the heavier the logistics trail, and the greater the number of vulnerabilities associated with supply operations. Trees may come to be better protected by sticking them in the forest rather than by building an obvious brick wall around them.

3. THE SHAPE OF WAR TO COME

Technology itself determines neither the shape nor the outcome of wars. Operations, geography, strategies, and rules of engagements play a large role in determining what works and what does not. Merely to list a few of the major questions is to illustrate how many assumptions are needed for even plausible forecasting.

Who will U.S. forces have to take the field against peer competitors, sophisticated mid-range opponents with and without peer help, unsophisticated clones of the former Soviet Union, and sophisticated but poor clones of Mao's forces? Will the next war be fought for limited objectives, or will we be forced to terminate the other side in order to terminate conflict? Will a conventional attack come as a surprise (whether deliberately or through an unplanned concatenation of events), or will the conventional phase be planned as the ultimate phase of a campaign whose early stages featured guerilla conflict? Where, and for which interests, will the United States get involved? What, if anything, will be off-limits—to us, to the other side? To what extent will the United States have to coerce the uninvolved in order to remove an information conduit to the other side? Will weapons of mass destruction be involved? Will we fight in alliances, in coalitions, or unilaterally?

What would we be fighting for (and thus what means would we use): to defend itself, but more often its friends (and other allies), preserve regional stability, inhibit the rise of a peer competitor, or keep lines of communications open (e.g., SLOCS, information infrastructure)?

If the odds of a direct clash with a major power are small, the most prototypical challenging situation is for the United States to face a technologically savvy (but not necessarily equally large), middle-income country (e.g., a national income 2 to 20 percent that of ours—a category that includes Japan circa 1941) seeking unwarranted coercive influence in its region. It is useful to remember that although few middle-income countries today possess much in the way of militaries, those that are aggressive are well armed (e.g., Syria, North Korea). Any of many middle-income countries that might turn ugly over 20 years will have had plenty of time to acquire militaries disproportionate to their incomes; thus the potential threat base is much larger than the threat base at any one time.

Adding to the stress is the possibility that the threat may enjoy the tacit support of another great power. The United States will have a tough time holding that power accountable if its support is dovert or if the evidence is ambiguous. The United States is limited in the casualties it will accept, the casualties it is willing to inflict on civilians (and even, as the reaction to media reports from the "Road of Death" illustrates, on other soldiers), and the casualties it is willing to put at risk (e.g., from WMD actions of the other side); the other side may well have few such limitations (other than as prudence dictates). One quick implication is that a war that trades life for life (even at fairly favorable ratios) may be a strategic defeat for the United States; one which trades equipment dollar for dollar (even at fairly unfavorable ratios) is more likely to result in a strategic victory. What can we say about the parameters of such a conflict, what are the limits of U.S. action, and how should the U.S. military be organized to meet such a challenge?

REFIGHTING THE LAST WAR

If something as complex as the U.S. role in the Gulf War can be summarized in six words they would be: ship in, cut talk, run wild. That is, we moved a mountain of material over a 5-month period to the Persian Gulf, used air power to destroy Iraq's communications, and then ran wild (first with bombers, then with tanks) over their miserable forces. These three are precisely what U.S. forces will be unable to do in the challenging scenario 20 years hence.

Ship In

Few doubt that U.S. forces will have to travel much farther to the next big battlefield than our foes will. Despite complaints over current organic lift assets, it is likely that one way or the other, U.S. forces will have to use lift to get there. Whether they will be able to survive doing so is another matter. Technology 20 years hence is threatening to make the littoral more hazardous. Surface ships are almost impossible to hide against the wide variety of organic and third-party surveillance assets available to even technologically unsophisticated foes. Doctrinally, most nations recognize that Iraq's allowing the United States time to deploy and organize was a major contributor to their defeat. Technically, a combination of very smart mine/torpedoes and saturation-type cruise or ballistic missile attacks could very well disable a nontrivial fraction of assets near shore; the only question is where between 10 and 1,000 kilometers from land the killing zone starts. Airlift may be more survivable because its exposure time is less, but relying on airlift limits the kind of assets that can be moved and such aircraft are, themselves, hardly stealthy; only if the foe is fastidious about not downing civilian aircraft are they likely to come in unchallenged.

Complex land targets such as ports and airfields are even more vulnerable than lift assets. Logistics dumps and command centers, however, may be tenable if they can be broken down into many little pieces; successful operations would then require a highly distributed information processing regime to overcome dispersion. If U.S. forces can also be spread out sufficiently widely, they may be able to ride out WMD attacks; however, dictates of geography (e.g., passes, isthmuses, valleys, islands) may prevent that strategy.

The up side of surface ship vulnerability comes from the potential shift from Europe to Asia as the cockpit of the world's wars. Islands and peninsulas dominate Asian far more than European geography. Thus for one Asian country to threaten another with invasion will more often require naval (or at very least widebody airlift) control, a far more difficult proposition when ships (and such aircraft) are as visible as they will be. Although Trojan Horse strategies (e.g., military assets masking as civilian ones) may work, they are self-defeating as threats for obvious reasons.

Cut Talk

Some theorists of information warfare see a coming bureaucratic conflict between those who would destroy an enemy's communications infrastructure and those who would keep enough intact so they could listen in. Unfortunately, despite Allied success in the Gulf, by 2014, we may not be able to do either.

Can counter-C2 warfare keep headquarters from talking to the troops? With every passing year the task becomes harder. A wireline system can be disabled by bombing central office switches. A distributed wireless system would be much less vulnerable, particularly if circuitry were reduced to sizes that could be placed on trucks or even in briefcases. Cellular transmissions leak, but decoy radiators can be constructed with ease. Furthermore, sidebands from microwave transmissions are easier to control.[8] Broadcasting digital messages to trusted relays in the field would provide an enemy another reliable method of communicating. He could also transmit on the sub-bands and blanking intervals of an uplink from a third-party live feed, such as a developing-world version of CNN; use focused transmissions from multiple ground sites through satellite terminals; or employ a public global cellular system, such as Iridium or Inmarsat-P. Compression allows messages to be multiplied on the same bandwidth. The technical details can be debated, but the means and density of global communications are constantly increasing, and finding a way of getting the message out is getting continually easier.

Indirect methods of attacking command and control systems via the power grid can currently cut the flow of information, but such techniques will have decreasing effect over the next 20 years. The Gulf War raised the perceived value of having considerable power backup for key military nodes if they face attack. If photovoltaic power continues to gain efficiency and to become less expensive (e.g., holographic films which may reach the critical 6 cents/kwh mark), a large part of a country's *total* power supply could be provided from sources too dispersed to target.

If American forces cannot interdict these possible communications flows, could they intercept and interpret them? This will become increasingly difficult, as well. Digital signals are inherently harder to intercept than analog ones. The combination of public key cryptography and triple-DES (data encryption standard) means that any digital point-to-point bit-stream can be rendered unreadable except by the party for whom it is intended. This will be true regardless of how powerful code-breaking computers become. Even if quantum computers, only a theory today, can be constructed they will not be available by 2015. The relative cost of using a larger encryption key is far smaller than the cost of breaking a message stream so encrypted. This is notwithstanding the U.S. Government's attempt to limit its spread via the Clipper chip, which permits encryption but leaves some official access to keys for decryption. The same technology used in digital signatures makes it virtually impossible to alter the source of a message or its content without having the receiver reject the message as corrupted. If applied to computer network operations, our ability to infiltrate a virus, worm, or "Trojan Horse" into an enemy network would be sharply curtailed.

True, the digitization of the global communications infrastructure will take decades. Even afterwards, human error will inevitably occur on the enemy side, insider assistance may be available to American forces, and source-level or destination-level eavesdropping would still yield useful information. Whatever American forces could learn would be helpful, but they should not expect to acquire a great deal of information from such sources in 2015.

Run Wild

It is a truism of the Gulf War that Allied forces used dominating maneuver to deliver the coup de grace to Iraq's force. The Left Hook put forces where Iraq did not expect them, and their immobilization made them sitting ducks. Advocates of maneuver warfare argue that, despite the increasing difficulties its execution may face over the next 20 years, it will still offer success to its practitioners in 2015. Moving forces are harder to strike than immobile forces and maneuver places them in a superior position from which to strike the enemy. Furthermore, the surprise that springs from maneuver can disorient opponents and reduce their well-laid plans to chaos.

But these arguments could carry far less force in 20 years. First, moving targets per se, are easier to hit. Movement generates far more signatures than immobility and few moving platforms can outrun precision weaponry. Rather than break a target lock, movement only may confirm it. As long as information generated by movement can be relayed to a weapon, its ability to strike will be maintained.

Second, range may be of decreasing importance in warfare. Sensor proliferation, especially when decoupled from platforms, as well as their increasing employment in space, means that target signatures will be acquired almost as easily from great as from small distances to targets. The greater the range, the greater the cost of landing steel on targets. But for high-value targets such as ships, armored vehicles, and aircraft, long-range strike remains cost-effective—given a $10,000 per kilogram cost of launching a GPS/INS-guided weapon from open ocean. Systems such as the Army Tactical Missile System (ATACMs) or emerging technologies such as electromagnetic rail-gun artillery may permit even more cost-effective strikes from closer but still-standoff distances.

Third, while humans will be as vulnerable to surprise and confusion 20 years out, silicon will be as invulnerable 20 years out as well. For the purposes of target acquisition (and perhaps target servicing) silicon is taking over more and more functions from humans. This transition will take place neither overnight nor completely (man-in-the-loop will remain and rules-of-engagement differ from war to war), but the trend is clear. In recent years the U.S. Army has developed new ways of producing concentration of firepower without concentration of forces. The fact remains that, against a sophisticated foe, the advantages of running wild have come and gone.

WAR IN 2015

If the Gulf War model is unlikely to retain its validity against a sophisticated foe, what might replace it? Perhaps a *look high, run low* model best describes what conventional war is coming to.

Look High

If sensor proliferation increases the information available to combatants, logic dictates a transition from local to global information loops in the ageless game of hide-and-seek. The difference between local and global loops may be illustrated by differences in mechanized warfare between 1991 and 2015.

In the local loop model as used in the Gulf War, the armor commander was provided with basic intelligence data on enemy location. He then found and destroyed targets on his own, using organic sensors. In the global loop model the search for the enemy would be conducted in real time by a wide variety of sensors—from space to air to ground, including sensors organic to the armored group. The inflow of data would be fused and then exploited by the armored force. Even in the 4 years since the Gulf War, the reliance upon direct visual sightings prior to target engagement has been slowly replaced by direct transmission of coordinates to tank or armored group. The logic of the Army's digital battlefield initiative still presumes that broadband information will be sent to the operator, rather than the operator being prosecutor of findings. As empowering as this presumption is to the soldier, it may not accord with the logic of future conflict. Giving every soldier access to the location of all friendly forces and individuals may yield a catastrophe if just one friendly node is turned.

Although the transition from local to global loops preceded the Gulf War (e.g., submarine warfare) and will still be incomplete after 2015 (e.g., SOF operations), the trends are clear. The side best capable of gathering, fuzing, and acting quickly on target information will, everything else being equal, do better.

As they become core practices of the American military over the next 20 years, sensor deployment and data fusion will require their own doctrine and concept of operations. Space-based systems, UAVs, mobile, over-the-horizon radar imaging and a wide variety of ground-based sensors will certainly play a larger role in tactical and operational situations than they do at present. Constructing the necessary communications links and deciding what information they transmit back to command and/or operational nodes (as opposed to what information is processed locally) will present an immense task. So would be the management of the information flood generated in an escalating crisis, as data from stand-off sensors increasingly will be supplemented by intrusive sensors.

In the mid-1990s, each service or subservice community acts on the basis of estimates formed by its own organic sensors. Even so, readings from different sensors primarily are fused so that one can back up the readings of others. Coordination and standardization alone are used to create information unity. This approach, which already showed strains in the Gulf War, is a vestige of a time when space operations were oriented to strategic ends and most information loops were local. It is not clear how well such a model would work as military space operations are redesigned to fit tactical and operational requirements and non-space-based sensors receive wider battlefield use. An Information Command or Corps may be needed to coordinate such functions effectively.

The separation of information processing and target prosecution has ramifications beyond those of internal Defense Department organization. If sending large forces overseas becomes increasingly difficult, how would the United States assist beleaguered allies? Bytes are far easier to move than bombs, bullets, and beans. The logic of information-based warfare would prescribe the functions of the members of vertical coalitions. Those under attack would provide the combat forces, as well as direct their emplacement, direction, and movement. The United States would provide the information systems to multiply the effectiveness of fighting forces. Easiest for the United States to provide would be the various data streams coming from our space and sea-based sensors. Next easiest would be software and systems integration to fuse all the data we would provide, along with the information collected by American allies. Simulation software for training and mission planning would fall in the same range of difficulty. The delivery of American sensors (those that could not be bought on the open market) would prove more difficult. Most difficult would be the delivery of American weapons themselves. Their shipment would expose U.S. forces to dangers similar to those that would be encountered in transporting a large force.

Vertical coalitions can overcome the two fundamental strategic weaknesses of U.S. operations: a greater sensitivity to casualties (compared to local forces) and a greater logistics challenge. There may also be times when we would like to help a friend but would be loathe to find ourselves responsible for harming the friend of another great power. Vertical coalitions offer, within bounds, the promise of being able to provide assistance while minimizing fingerprints as well as footprints.

Such a scheme has its drawbacks. For an ally, a vertical coalition is always a second-best alternative; nothing says long-term commitment like spilled American blood on foreign soil. Donated data are never as trusted as organic information. What we consider important information may not accord to the realities on the ground, or to their doctrine. Finding out whether or why target estimates proved to be false negatives or false positives will be difficult without our people in country. Interoperability will be a major concern, as will be the risk of letting any other country understand how our systems work to the degree necessary to make vertical coalitions possible. Still, second-best may be the best we have left, given the difficulties of projecting surface forces.

Run Low

Contemporary conventional warfare centers on platforms containing operator, weapon, sensor, and emitter, but the logic of such platform design will diminish by 2015. A multitude of sensors would allow precision in targeting and will generate overlapping and reinforcing readings, but a commensurate multiplication of platforms would be highly expensive to produce and would risk huge casualties if engaged. Detached weapons fired by remote control would generate far less signature than similar activity by platforms. If such weapons were destroyed before use, the human consequences would be greatly diminished. However, there are two great disadvantages to a distributed weapons architecture. First, they require more movement of individual unprotected items into position. Second, they send and receive information in a deliberately noisy electromagnetic environment.

When two sophisticated opponents confront each other in conventional war the result is likely to be not a rapid clash of arms but a slow motion test of competing information systems. The side that tries to start operations by the sudden and violent eruption of platforms will find its weaponry picked off and blown to pieces by hidden missiles linked directly to sensor systems and impervious to shock. The real trick is to find out exactly what the other side sees. Barring direct observation (e.g., infiltrators), the next best method is to bait with various worms and see which fish bite. For instance, an enemy may know in advance that the United States possesses weaponry that homes in on the sound of a tank coupled with infrared signatures. Can it devise a warm noisy decoy that will attract attack or are their other signatures that are needed to induce an attack? Will the weapon be fired against individual tanks or does it wait for a tank column? Conversely, would attackers be advised to let some talks roll unimpeded in hopes that the enemy builds a false confidence that it has fooled the system?

In such circumstances, war could become very slow (after all the interesting assets impossible to hide have been reduced to rubble) as both sides try to keep their equipment signatures beneath the envelope that signals identification; most of the successful engagements may affect the occasional but fatal mistakes that show up as live targets. As noted, it is not necessary that equipment signatures be reduced to below noise level; it may suffice to reduce signatures of military equipment to where they can be confused with signatures of civilian equipment.

Such an environment would be ideal for special operations forces; their training accustoms them to minimizing their signatures. Furthermore, the vertical coalitions previously described could depend on direct human support from U.S. special forces and would provide tangible evidence of U.S. engagement, protect key intelligence assets, and report back on how information systems were really performing, rather than what our allies might want us to believe. Even if human participation in combat could not be eliminated, it could be minimized in a way that radically altered the nature of American intervention in foreign conflict.

Does this mean that the U.S. Armed Forces can dispense with firepower and platforms altogether? Not by 2015. After being retrofitted with some new information technologies, our platforms would remain capable of exerting tremendous force against less sophisticated foes. Against an enemy with sophisticated information-based systems, however, U.S. forces would find themselves at great risk. In any conflict, we could rely on our stand-off weapons including long-range stealth bombers, cruise missiles and perhaps hyperkinetic artillery; however, in the most likely conflicts in which the United States might become engaged in 20 years, we would employ our information-based systems first and follow with weapon platforms only if necessary.

4. CONCLUSIONS AND IMPLICATIONS

In 1915, the enraged American reaction to the sinking of *Lusitania* by a German U-Boat first raised the possibility that the United States might become engaged in the Great War and be required to send an Allied Expeditionary Force across the Atlantic.

2015 will mark the centennial of that event. Will the era of heavy intervention forces be over? Most military assets, particularly those large enough to wield powerful weaponry, will be too visible to survive long in the information-based warfare environment previously described. Will there be any defense interests between now and 2015 that would justify very high casualty rates? How many casualties would the American public tolerate before calling for a review of tactical nuclear options?

Even if heavy intervention is abjured, the United States will be able play a large role in international security. Look-high capabilities will permit American forces and, more so, those of American allies to operate far more effectively than their foes. In some cases, particularly when helping an ally defend his territory against encroachment, such American capabilities may prove decisive. In other cases, however, such as defending civilian commerce, recovering territory or overcoming a military disadvantage created by subversion or deception, our relative advantage may be nullified by unfavorable military circumstances.

But despite the imperatives created by the technological developments described in this section, the United States may not reorganize, re-equip, and retrain its forces appropriately. Selfish bureaucratic interests may resist such changes successfully. Nor is it likely that the United States will become engaged in a war between now and 2015 that would teach the harsh lessons for the need for such changes. Thus, a significant dissonance may develop between American military needs and military realities. Several policy-related implications flow from the influences of the information-based military-technical revolutions on American and foreign military forces.

PROGRAMMING

If weapon platforms are declining rapidly in utility, purchasing more of them makes little sense. Initiating a major development cycle to manufacture more tomorrow makes even less sense. Platform-centric organizations may place faith in stealth to maintain the viability of their weapon systems. Unfortunately, stealthy platforms are expensive, difficult to maintain, and usable only under certain circumstances, such as night flying. Furthermore, some platforms, such as surface combatants, are inherently unstealthy. The application of stealth probably should be limited to submarines, some bombers and special operations equipment. There may be some virtue in retrofitting existing equipment with stealth technology to reduce their signatures, but purchasing entirely new systems to achieve the same result is not cost effective. In any event, today's stringent budgeting environment has eliminated most major acquisition systems, with the proper exception of information-intensive systems and munitions that can incorporate new information technologies. Insofar as platform inventories will shape American force structure, the replacement of conventional warfare units by information-based warfare units will follow.

PARTNERS

Where the costs of projecting a large surface force is deemed too expensive, the United States will have to find new ways to provide military support to its allies. In that case, besides standoff and special operations, our interventions could involve contributions of bytes than battle formations. But forming such vertical coalitions would present both political and technological challenges. The former would entail persuading actual and potential allies that the terms for American military engagement had changed. As a carrot, the United States could argue that its military contributions, while far less visible, would be sufficiently valuable to warrant our participation in the planning for war and war termination. As a stick, the United States could very well explain that, in the absence of major threats to our vital national interests, American assistance would be provided only on a take-it-or-leave-it basis.

The technical dimensions of such cooperation would be daunting. We would have to solve the difficult problems of systems engineering to ensure that our information-generating systems and their information reception systems could communicate fully. Given the enormous difficulties, perhaps impossibility, of ad hoc systems engineering, the United States justifiably might begin establishing standards for interoperability now, so that other nations have the option of developing systems that could mate with ours in 10 to 20 years. We also would have to resolve doctrinal and operational issues to ensure that the information we would provide would be both trusted and suited to a partner's method of warfare.

PRESENCE

The prepositioning of military forces might seem the solution to the problems of overseas intervention. But foreign bases do not obviate the requirement for logistics. No overseas American forces currently are sufficient to mount a credible and sustainable defense of their positions without a major, thus visible, source of supplies and manpower. Large bases are themselves visible and vulnerable targets. But replacing conventional U.S. forces with special operations and standoff forces would be inhibited by the negative political and psychological influence on the morale of our local allies and thus would undermine the cohesion of the alliance. At the same time, information-based warfare increases the requirement for American overseas presence. As noted, the ability to interoperate our military information systems with an ally's is facilitated by intimate knowledge of how the ally operates, ranging from technical specifications to operational considerations. Finally, the presence of U.S. forces in an allied country would facilitate greatly the placing and maintaining sensors as a cooperative effort. Consequently, while American military presence overseas would retain its value, the form and context of this presence must be adopted to the shifting parameters of conventional warfare.

IMPLICATIONS FOR MILITARY ORGANIZATION

Technology suggests alternative military organizations; it may permit them but it cannot compel them. Whether or not the U.S. Armed Forces adapt to information technologies will depend on bureaucratic forces, whatever tasks it is called on to do over the next 20 years, and the laws of chance. The same goes for foreign armed forces. That said, the following changes logically follow from advances in information technology.

First, technology's ability to shrink the loop between target detection and engagement puts a premium on similarly quick command-and-control structures. Clearly the middle layers need to shrink, but should decisionmaking fall to the bottom or rise to the top? The former is in vogue; put unit commanders in charge, and enable them to command strike forces from a wide menu. The latter permits commanders to exercise "rudder controls" from over-the-horizon. Relegating more chunks of the decision to automated systems may free up the commander to devote more energy to the strategic side of warfighting. With expert systems, alternative courses of action (including the pre-assignment of targets to shooters) may be established for operational units; decisions on which to employ could be modified on the fly as battlefield exigencies dictate.

Although organization must reflect circumstances (e.g., steppe and jungle engagements are fought differently), the push-data-up model may emerge simply because the opportunities for U.S. forces to fight close-in during high-intensity engagements are going away. The greater the concentration on standoff weapons, the more a centralized model makes sense.

Second, managing the sensor-to-shooter cycle may require a corps specialized for that task. An information corps, as such, would make fundamental decisions about the deployment of sensors, build and maintain the command-and-control links necessary to keep them operational, construct and update the software that converts individual readings into a coherent whole, manage the process by which readings are converted into fire-control solutions, and oversee whatever advanced training and learning tools (e.g., simulation) are needed to help users work the system. There will still be a role for commanders; indeed command will still be central to any warfighting detail. However, the management of information systems will be devolved.

Third, by contrast, the day of the mass military against sophisticated foes may be coming to an end in two senses. First, the agglomeration of platforms (e.g., think of D-Day), and the various signatures attendant to such agglomerations will be inadvisable in tomorrow's warfare environment. Indeed, if large platforms are of decreasing utility, so will organizations built around them. Second, whether the subject be a information corps tending to software, special operators tending to threats in their environment, or anything in between, the information environment of every military operative will differ more and more over time—everyone will be solving different problems with less and less relationship to each other. Information differentiates functionality. With every advance in technology, the number of different skill categories proliferates. Uniformity—the historic basis of military organizations—may be harder to find.

NOTES

1. These include infrared, imaging infrared, television, visual, and fiber optic visual systems.

2. The greater availability and lower costs of new alloys, as well as the development of metal-ceramic matrix composites, will allow for missile weight reduction.

3. Such a sensor is so powerful that, if placed over Tokyo, it could distinguish between two fireflies flitting 3 meters apart over the Pentagon.

4. Clementine's visible-light sensor can photograph a 1.5 by 1.0 kilometer area with accuracy to 4 meters from a 200-kilometer-high orbit.

5. Boeing's space plane would launch and land horizontally. Lockheed/Rocketdyne's wedge-shaped spacecraft would launch vertically and land horizontally. The McDonnell-Douglas DC-X, closest to realization, would launch and land vertically.

6. The United States did not degrade GPS to accommodate our operations in Somalia, even though we and our U.N. allies faced considerable armed opposition there.

7. One novel approach could be a decoy generating a signal approximating the Side Aperture Radar (SAR) of a target.

8. Even our opponents in Somalia in 1993-94 managed to exploit the echoing properties of radio to hide the source of their transmissions. We are likely to face far more technological sophistication in 2015, even in the poorest of developing countries.

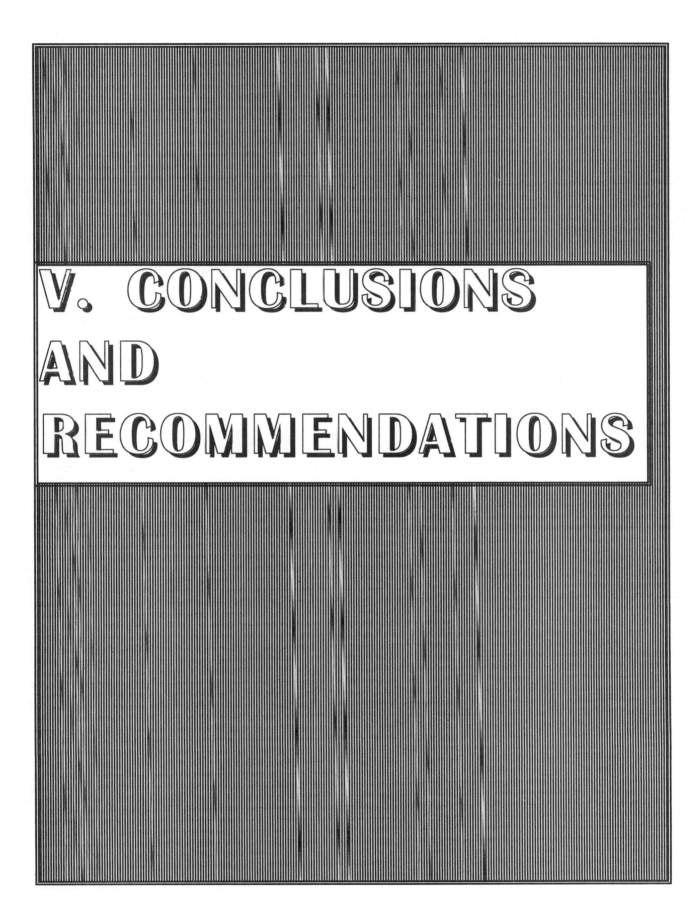

V. CONCLUSIONS AND RECOMMENDATIONS

1. CONCLUSIONS

With the end of the Cold War, the United States has begun a new period in its history. The country has entered a fourth era of national security policy. In the first period, the United States defended and preserved its new independence based on a "perpetual" alliance with France. But the permanent linking of their country's fortune to the affairs of Europe left many Americans uneasy. In 1793, fear of being drawn into European conflicts led George Washington to abrogate the alliance. With that, the United States began the long period of isolationism from Europe, broken only by the First World War and Woodrow Wilson's brief flirtation with the League of Nations concept. During the century and a half of Isolationism, the United States did prosper thanks to its geographical separation from the quarrels of the great powers, liberal immigration policies and exploitation of the immense resources of North America. By the eve of World War II, the country had grown from a weak, sparsely populated agricultural state into the richest and potentially most powerful country in the world.

The attack on Pearl Harbor forced Americans to abandon Isolationism. In December 1941, the United States began what would become a 50-year struggle to prevent totalitarian powers from achieving world supremacy. After victory in World War II, most Americans would have preferred to return to Isolationism, but the new Soviet threat forced the United States to come to the defense of Western Europe and Eastern Asia. Despite several bitter wars and intermittent periods of weariness, the United States maintained its commitments for over 40 years.

The collapse of the Soviet empire unexpectedly brought to a close the long struggle to defend the United States and its allies from aggression. Feeling secure from this victory, some Americans favored slashing national security expenditures and turning inward to concentrate on domestic problems, but the outbreak of various conflicts in the immediate post-Cold War years, as well as global economic interdependence, made clear the disadvantages of such retreat. The American people realized that they would have to engage their power to maintain a degree of world stability. Furthermore, the products of the huge American economy could no longer be absorbed by the domestic market alone. Economic necessity had intertwined American interests with those of the global population. The United States had to conduct its national security policy accordingly. The end of the Cold War, however, had altered fundamentally the position of the United States in the world. As a result, the American people now face a question unique in their history. As citizens of the world's single superpower, they are free to follow a completely active, rather than a defensive, national security policy. But what goals should they pursue? How should they achieve them? To begin answering those questions, they must anticipate the dangers and opportunities that lie before them.

Readers will have noted the curious absence of the United States from many of the speculations made in this study. Surely the United States would prevent some of the more threatening developments described from taking place. This omission of American action is deliberate, to accentuate the consequences both of American action and inaction over the next 20 years. In a world of great powers, the United States must act or submit to being acted upon. Yet when the United States would employ its might, it would likely be most effective within a coalition or alliance. Group action would greatly increase American diplomatic clout and provide the practical and symbolic advantages conferred by collective security arrangements. However, to function well, alliances and coalitions require compromise by their members, even the strongest. To avoid having its enormous power perceived as threatening by its partners or by the international community, the United States must employ it in a restrained and cooperative manner. Paradoxically, the American people must practice a degree of self-restraint in order to reach the aims of a reasonable national security policy.

This study also argues that many of the dire predictions about resource and environmental catastrophe predicted for the next two decades could overstate the dangers to American interests. This is not to deny that tens millions of people may suffer dreadfully from want in coming decades. *2015* suggests that the United States and other great powers may command the means to mitigate such tragedies, but they may rarely need the intervention of combat forces to deal with such crises. Despite rapid population growth over the next twenty years, resulting pressures are unlikely to overwhelm American ability to respond effectively. When the United States does, it could do so primarily by nonviolent means, as directed by prudent policy .

War will likely remain a danger to the human race over the next 20 years. Because of the increasing accuracy of weaponry, warfare may wreak ever more havoc, even without the employment of weapons of mass destruction. Yet if the arguments made in chapter four prove correct, the defense may prove superior to the offense should wars be waged by advanced powers in the early twenty-first century. This shift in the type of warfare would present severe challenges to American national security. In the 19th century, the United States rose to a position of world power while shielded by a period of defense-dominant warfare. When in 1917 the United States intervened militarily in the affairs of the great powers, it coincided with the offense regaining the advantage in warfare. This period in military history may be coming to an end. If future decades present ever-greater obstacles to projecting forces against technologically sophisticated hostile states, the United States would find it increasingly difficult to intervene abroad. In order to protect its interests and to deter aggression, the United States would have to invent new strategic, operational and tactical concepts—as well as the innovative weapons and equipment to wage such warfare.

Despite such potential problems, this study strongly suggests the wisdom of taking an active role in world affairs. It strongly suggests the wisdom of preventing potential problems, rather than reacting to them only after they materialize. To a great extent, this requires a new approach to maintaining the security of the United States that is neither isolationist, defensive, or confrontational.

No one can yet characterize the next era in American national security policy. That must wait until national aims have been agreed upon, the obstacles to them identified, and the measures to overcome them devised. Once the shape of future policy has become clearer, its major features will suggest its name. The new era likely will be identified by the anxieties, the sense of limits, and the recognition of international responsibilities that have replaced the brief euphoria of 1989-91.

The majority of the American people currently still support a range of U.S. engagement across the globe. Yet they are increasingly concerned by the stagnation or decline in the economic and social well-being of the majority of their fellow citizens. Domestic realities necessarily influence national security policy. Still, *2015* indicates the dangers of U.S. inaction abroad, however attractive such detachment might appear to those who prefer to focus on domestic issues. In the past, the American people have dealt successfully with major internal and external problems simultaneously. Certainly they possess the energy, determination, and ingenuity to do so again. As a rough guide to how they might best apply such resources to the challenges that may face them beyond the borders of the United States, the authors of *2015* offer the following recommendations.

2. RECOMMENDATIONS

1: Prepare to confront opponents more challenging than mid-size regional powers. The present focus on two nearly simultaneous Major Regional Contingencies is based on the international situation of the early 1990s. In coming decades, the American defense planners should consider the possibility of confrontation with a technologically sophisticated major power. By or beyond 2015, the United States might face a hostile great power, even a hostile great power coalition. Such questions might be considered during the quadrennial strategy review recommended by the Roles and Missions Commission.

2: De-emphasize large military platforms as the basis for force structure, organizing forces and devising operational concepts and plans. Rapidly developing sensor and weapon technology make large military platforms easier to detect, track, target, and destroy. By 2015 large military platforms as we know them today likely will be approaching an untenable level of vulnerability on the battlefield. Therefore, in planning for the future they probably should not occupy the central place they do today in the arsenals of leading military powers nor play a dominant role in the organization and operations of military forces. It is unrealistic for the United States to shed all of its large military platforms within the next two decades: some will continue to be useful against less sophisticated foes, information-technology upgrades will improve their performance, and stealth will provide varying degrees of survivability. However, long-term recapitalization of the armed forces should not concentrate on iterative improvement of the large military platforms, organization and operational concepts of the past. The future for United States military forces is to be able to see, understand and strike an enemy without giving him anything vital to exploit, corrupt or destroy. This will drive military force structure toward a mix rich in networked sensors and information processors, long-range precision weapons. A force possessing robust capacity to move into crisis areas but not necessarily having to enter combat zones to engage the enemy. A flat organization of highly trained, specialized forces possessing distributed firepower capable of operating independently or in conjunction with indigenous forces.

3: Increase information sharing and training with allies and potential coalition partners. Increased information sharing and training could help the United States maintain its lead in information-based warfare, improve interoperability with allies and facilitate creation of *ad hoc* coalitions. To the extent feasible, the United States should develop technologies and doctrine to support vertical coalitions. In these, local forces would supply more of the firepower and infrastructure, Americans would

---

provide more of the information, associated systems and stand-off weapons. Thus, the United States should be preparing its allies to make the best use of the weapons it alone can offer them. But it must remain prepared to defend with American combat forces those allies too weak to do so themselves. On the other hand, the United States also should begin planning for contingencies when long-standing security relationships may prove of limited utility and new ones need to be created.

AFTERWORD

This study does not predict the outbreak of another world war, nor does it argue the inevitability of the rise of a future peer military competitor with the United States. However, *2015* does emphasize the crucial importance over the next two decades of channeling the competition among the great powers in non-violent directions. To do so necessarily requires educated guesses about the ongoing changes in warfare.

How much will the global security environment alter between 1996 and 2015? The warfare and weapons of 2015 conceivably could present little more than evolutionary developments of what was witnessed in the Persian Gulf War of 1991. Furthermore, war between great powers may not occur anywhere in the world. Instead, the major states may well pursue their interests and settle their differences in peaceful ways. Today's principal alliances may endure. Failed and outlaw states may remain the central concern of American defense contingency planning.

But the international situation in 2015 could differ sharply from that of 1986 or 1996. At least some of the great powers could be locked in an increasingly antagonistic relationship, making the problems of the developing world seem relatively insignificant as far as American national security was concerned. *Ad hoc* coalitions might supplant permanent alliances in importance. Increasing numbers of medium powers might be gaining access to information technologies with military applications and to precision-deliverable weapons of mass destruction. In other words, the world of 2015 could be one of far less certainty than that of the Cold War and of far greater danger than that which the United States faces at present. We find this latter world view plausible and one that offers a far more prudent basis for American defense planning in the late 1990s.

ABOUT THE EDITOR

Patrick M. Cronin is a Senior Fellow at the National Defense University's Institute for National Strategic Studies, where he directs the Asia-Pacific affairs research team. Dr. Cronin also serves a Professorial Lecturer in international relations at the Paul H. Nitze School of Advanced International School of Advanced International Studies, The Johns Hopkins University, as well as Associate Editor of the journal, *Strategic Review*. Prior to joining the University, he held research positions at the Center for Naval Analyses, SRI International, and the Congressional Research Services. Dr. Cronin, earned his master's and doctoral degrees at Oxford University, served as the overall editor for this study.

ISBN 0-16-048752-8